HEALTHY 中醫
SMOOTHIES

Traditional Chinese Medicine Inspired Recipes

Ancient Traditions ☯ Modern Healing

By Kimberly Ashton & Zhang Yifang

Better Link Press

This book is edited and designed by the Editorial Committee of *Cultural China* series

Text: Kimberly Ashton, Zhang Yifang

Photography, Food & Beverage Styling: Rosa Chen

Production Assistants, Recipe Testers & Stylists: Cheryl Lin, Franziska von Wahl, Vivian Wu,
    Jieli Xie, April Zhu, Georgia Zhou

Cover and Interior Design: Wang Wei

Copy Editor: Gretchen Zampogna

Editors: Wu Yuezhou, Yang Xiaohe

Editorial Director: Zhang Yicong

Senior Consultants: Sun Yong, Wu Ying, Yang Xinci

Managing Director and Publisher: Wang Youbu

ISBN: 978-1-60220-155-2

Address any comments about *Healthy Smoothies: Traditional Chinese Medicine Inspired Recipes* to:

Better Link Press

99 Park Ave

New York, NY 10016

USA

or

Shanghai Press and Publishing Development Company

F 7 Donghu Road, Shanghai, China (200031)

Email: comments_betterlinkpress@hotmail.com

Printed in China by Shenzhen Donnelley Printing Co., Ltd.

1   3   5   7   9   10   8   6   4   2

Contents

Facing page
Summer treats: rosebud nut milk and yellow watermelon mint refresher.

Facing page

Nourishing barley, power vitamin C charged sea buckthorn, with refresing mint, apple and carrot.

Chapter One
The Basics of Traditional Chinese Medicine

Food is a part of everyday life, so much so that you may not give it a great deal of thought. Food offers an incredible ability to heal and nourish the human body. Different foods and herbs can act like medicine in their positive effects and help sustain a healthy state over time. Since they can produce a wide range of results, and at times even harmful effects, foods should be considered and chosen carefully so as to lead to greater well-being. This attitude toward food's many, and varied, effects, is at the core of Chinese medical diet therapy.

1. A Holistic Approach

Food combines with the clear water we drink and the pure air we breathe, forming one of the strongest links between the universe and us. *Tian ren xiang ying*, a Chinese proverb, denotes that relevant adaptation of the human body to its natural environment is principal to keeping the human body healthy and constantly healing itself.

The basics of good food and personalized nutrition based on the individual's constitution are very important in Traditional Chinese Medicine (TCM), but equally important is a holistic approach. A holistic approach means TCM focuses on the organic whole of the person, physiologically and psychologically, from head to toe, to bring the individual in balance with nature and society. It emphasizes using natural remedies—food and herbs—as well as adjusting the mind, before treating with medicine, because this approach helps us find the root cause of the unbalance, rather than just focusing on the symptoms.

Just as the old saying goes, an ounce of prevention is worth a pound of cure. The preventative side of TCM provides an appealing and accessible point of entry for anyone who wants to learn about and use Chinese medicine. Food therapy is the easiest way to start. Using plants and foods for health and the prevention of illness is deeply ingrained in China's rich culture.

2. Yin-Yang Theory and the Application to Food

Yin and yang is an ancient philosophical concept that is central to

TCM. Yin and yang are two fundamental principles or forces in the universe, ever opposing and supplementing each other. All things and phenomena in the natural world contain two opposite components of yin and yang; for example, heaven and earth or heat and cold.

Yin and Yang

We should now step back a moment and explore the basic concept of yin and yang more thoroughly. In the beginning, yin and yang described a physical or geographical location in relation to the sun. A place exposed to the sun is yang, and a place without exposure is yin. The southern side of a mountain, for example, is yang, while its northern side is yin. Thus the ancient Chinese people, in the course of their everyday lives and work, came to understand that all aspects of the natural world could be seen as having a dual aspect: for example, day and night, brightness and dimness, movement and stillness, upward and downward. The terms yin and yang were applied to express these dual and opposite qualities.

In TCM, yin and yang properties can be assigned to one's constitution as well as the food and herbs one consumes. A yang constitution includes hot, dry and overly strong properties of different body systems, while yin constitutions demonstrate cold, damp and weak properties. Yin foods, such as watermelon and mung bean, can bring nourishment and moisture internally as well as to the skin and orifices. They can reduce heat and calm the mind. Yang foods, such as walnut and cinnamon, can warm and energize the body, dry dampness and stimulate metabolism. Neutral foods, such as mushrooms, provide nutrition without influencing body systems.

TCM uses food to balance constitutions. For example, if a person's constitution has too much yang, it can be neutralized by yin food, and vice versa.

The Temperature of Foods and Herbs

Let's examine what is we mean by yang and yin foods and herbs.

Yang means the "temperature" of the food is warm or hot; this is an inherent property and not necessarily dependent on the surface temperature of the food.

Yang foods are more likely to be seasonal foods found in the winter. Things like root vegetables (beetroots, parsnips, squash, mustard, burdock and Chinese yams) are great for warming and grounding us during the colder months. Cooking or preparation methods include stir-frying, stewing, baking, deep-frying, roasting, grilling and barbecuing. These foods and herbs make our body energy rise and come to the surface.

Yin means the temperature of the food is cool or cold, and the taste is sour, bitter or salty. These foods are found most plentifully in the summer, and are often eaten raw or steamed. Yin foods restrain our body's energy or cause it to descend. Some examples include sprouts, asparagus, grapefruit, avocado and leafy green vegetables.

There are also a lot of foods that have very mild yin or yang qualities, and therefore belong to the "neutral" food category. Examples include rice, corn, beetroots, Chinese yams, kale and carrots. Even if you do not have detailed knowledge about the yin and yang of food, you can quite naturally get a balance of yin and yang by consuming a broad range of foods and ensuring variety. In times of illness or imbalance, learning about and applying food therapy will help you nourish your organs and energy.

3. The Chinese Concept of Qi and Blood

In traditional Chinese culture, qi is a fundamental concept and it is a part of everything that exists. It is everywhere in all the wonders of the universe. Everything you can see, feel and experience contains qi. It is the energy, vitality or life-process that flows in and around all of us.

Qi is created from oxygen inhaled during the breathing process, food essence and original qi that you are born with. The lungs play a very important role in this process because your breathing processes enrich your qi. Without good breathing habits, the quality and quantity of qi can be affected.

The idea of food essence comes from the TCM concept of the spleen, which refers to the group of organs with digestive functions, including the spleen, pancreas and part of small intestine. The spleen transforms and transports your nutrients into "clear qi." You are born with an original qi, which is stored in your kidneys.

Blood is one of the essential substances that makes up the human body and maintains the life activities. It is a red fluid that flows in the vessels, rich in nutrition. Blood is inseparable from qi, and qi infuses life into blood. However, blood is much denser, and unlike qi, it cannot change into an invisible form. The spleen, lung, heart and kidney organ systems are vital for the production of blood.

4. Five Elements Theory and the "Taste"

In Chinese, the Five Elements are called *wu xing: wu* means five and *xing* means movement and change. The Five Elements— wood, fire, earth, metal and water—have their own specific properties, but they also play interactive functions of generation and restriction. For example, earth generates metal but restricts water, while earth, in turn, is restricted by wood. This means that the relationship between the elements is one of constant motion and change.

The therapeutic use of food in TCM is partly based on the Five Elements model, as each food or herb has a certain "taste" related to one of the elements. Five Elements theory also states that each of the tastes has certain effects on the body, as described below. The "taste" of a food or herb is not always related to its flavor. For instance, broccoli is classified as "bitter" and millet as "salty." Taste, therefore, relates more to an intrinsic quality, rather than actual flavor, although the two will coincide in most cases.

Sour. This taste helps with digestive absorption, resisting fatty foods and preventing indigestion. It generates fluids and yin, while stopping discharge, perspiration, chronic cough and diarrhea. It also has an astringent effect on emissions, including sperm and frequent urine. It helps our bodies consolidate essential substances and prevents them from escaping. Sour foods can also bring disordered qi back to normal. Modern research shows sour flavors to be generally cleansing and detoxifying. However, we have to limit intake when ulcers or stones are present.

Bitter. This taste clears away heat, calms, hardens and dries dampness. It can control abnormally ascending qi and purge any pathogenic fire effect. In certain combinations, it can also improve the body's yin. Bitter foods can be used to treat most cases of excess and acute damp-heat or heat-fire. These foods should be limited if a weakness of qi and blood is present.

Sweet. Serving to nourish, moisten, moderate and invigorate the body, sweet foods can also regulate qi, blood, and function of the viscera. They strengthen any deficiency or symptoms and alleviate dryness. Sweet foods work in coordination with the spleen and stomach. They can help relieve pain and spasms, and reduce cough, ulcer and constipation. An excess of sweets should be avoided when suffering from damp, phlegm and water retention conditions.

Spicy (pungent). This taste disperses and promotes movement of qi and blood circulation. It stimulates digestion and helps break through blockage. It treats syndromes of the exterior, and expels stagnation of qi, blood and pathogens. Spicy foods must be used carefully, as many people cannot tolerate them.

Salty. These foods can promote moisture and have a softening effect. In particular, they regulate the moisture balance flowing downward in the body. They also move qi downward, increase urine and bowel movements, and are used to treat constipation and swelling. They promote the action of the kidney system, which allows beneficial foods to be fully absorbed and functional, and also improves concentration. Salty foods soften nodes and masses, and disperse accumulations in hardening muscles and glands.

Bland. This taste promotes urination and treats edema.

Together, the concepts of yin-yang and the Five Elements form the basis of traditional Chinese medical theory. They help explain the functions and relationships of different parts of the body, and guide clinical diagnosis and treatment. They also provide a wonderful guide to apply food therapy.

5. Knowing Your Constitution

What exactly is a constitution? How can it be influenced by food choice?

Constitution in TCM

Body constitution comprises our physical state, including the function of our internal systems and metabolism, together with our mental and spiritual states. As we pass through life, everyone's body constitution experiences periods of relative balance and imbalance, passing, for example, from hot to cold or dry to damp. Imbalance of our body constitutions could mark a transitional stage, when we are shifting away from health towards disorder, while not yet having a disease. Therefore, maintaining balance of body constitution can prevent or lessen disease and promote recovery from sickness. Traditional Chinese Medicine strives to balance the body's constitution, mitigate shocks from the outside environment, and dissolve toxic substances within our body.

The features of one's constitution can be detected in three areas: the person's physical build, the body's internal functions and the psychological state. It also depends on the stage of life the person is facing, such as puberty or menopause.

The constitution has two origins: congenital natural disposition and post-natal lifestyle (i.e. nature and nurture). Many factors influence the formation of the constitution, for instance: the parents' health, physically and mentally, at the time of conception, or the mother's condition during pregnancy. These parts belong to the congenital natural disposition of one's constitution.

However, most of the influence comes from our own actions and lifestyles. We can examine these with many factors, but food is one of the most important—and there are actually three contributing categories.

The first is basic healthy food that helps our body **maintain** itself on a daily basis. The second is food for **pleasure, relaxing, socializing** and as a response to satisfying certain emotional moods (in moderation, of course). The last is for the purpose of **healing**, reducing risks of illness, and maintaining and promoting good health. Modern nutritional science is now, more than ever, researching this last category, as our bodies fight to stay in good health in a fast-paced and changing world. However, "functional food" or medicinal food, as we call this last category, has had a very long history in TCM.

A Self-Assessment

To achieve balance and longevity, it is paramount to understand one's constitution and the factors that influence it. The basis of TCM is rooted in this understanding, which is then used to create treatment plans that will bring one's health to an optimal level. These highly individualized remedies include changing lifestyle habits and diet, as well as taking supplements. A person must understand his or her own constitution in order to take the right steps to find good health. The assessments below will help you learn more about your own constitution in order to choose foods and herbs specifically suited to your individual needs and for blending into delicious smoothies.

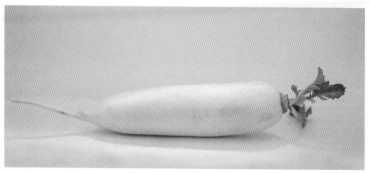

Reclining radish: great for detox and removing dampness in the body.

Questions Relating to Temperature

To determine Neutral, Cold, Hot or Mixed Constitutions

1) Are you sensitive to the cold or heat?

☐ normal (1)
☐ sensitive to cold (2)
☐ sensitive to heat (3)

2) What do you prefer to drink?

☐ depends on season (1)
☐ warm/hot drinks (2)
☐ cold drinks (3)

3) Do you sweat a lot?

☐ normal (1)
☐ less than average (2)
☐ more than average (3)

4) How do you classify your thirst?

☐ normal (1)
☐ not often thirsty (2)
☐ often thirsty (3)

5) How is your complexion?

☐ shining and rosy (1)
☐ pale and puffy (2)
☐ flushed (3)

6) How is your tongue coating when you get up in the morning?

☐ thin white fur (1)
☐ thick white fur (2)
☐ thick yellow fur (3)

7) What is your pulse (beats per minute)?

☐ from 60 to 80 (1)
☐ less than 60 (2)
☐ over 80 (3)

8) Do you drink tea or coffee?

☐ up to two cups of coffee or tea every day (1)
☐ three or more cups of tea every day (2)
☐ three or more cups of coffee every day (3)

9) What kind of food do you prefer?

☐ depends on season (1)

☐ a light taste or raw food (2)

☐ spicy or strongly flavored (3)

Assessment and your constitution:

Neutral: 6 or more responses of (1)

Cold: 6 or more of (2)

Hot: 6 of more of (3)

Mixed: if fewer than 6 of any one response

Questions Regarding Your Response to Adversity

To determine Neutral, Weak, Overly Strong or Mixed Constitutions

1) How energetic do you feel?

☐ average (1)

☐ more than average (2)

☐ less than average (3)

2) What is your tongue like when you get up in the morning?

☐ pink body and thin fur (1)

☐ dark or purple body and thick fur (2)

☐ pale or deeper red body and no fur (3)

3) What kind of food you prefer?

☐ mixed, with more vegetables and less meat (1)

☐ mostly meat (2)

☐ vegetarian (3)

4) How often is your elimination?

☐ normal (1)

☐ infrequent (2)

☐ too frequent (3)

5) How often do you get a cold every year?

☐ once or a few times (1)

☐ never (2)

☐ often (3)

6) How often do you get excited?

☐ normal (1)
☐ frequently (2)
☐ seldom (3)

7) How do your muscles feel?

☐ normal (1)
☐ tight and sore (2)
☐ soft and weak (3)

8) How quickly do you feel shortness of breath when hiking?

☐ 15 minutes to half an hour (1)
☐ more than half an hour (2)
☐ after a few minutes (3)

9) How does your head often feel?

☐ normal (1)
☐ pressure or sharp headache (2)
☐ lightheaded or dizziness (3)

Assessment and your constitution:

Neutral:	6 or more responses of (1)
Overly Strong:	6 or more of (2)
Weak:	6 or more of (3)
Mixed:	if fewer than 6 of any one response weak or overly strong

Choosing Food according to Your Constitution

In completing the above self-assessment, we encounter some pairs of concepts: cold or hot, weak or overly strong. Those two pairs are very useful when we apply food therapy. All these feelings, when within a certain range, are normal for us to feel; we should feel cold in winter and hot in summer. However, if we always feel cold, even in spring, or feel cold too often, then we should seek the underlying reason or root cause, and try to remedy it. Therefore, we should stay in neutral as long and often as we can and strive for balance. Below is how we match body types with a healthful diet:

Choosing different foods according to your constitution.

- Cold person: Add warming foods in moderation.
- Hot person: Add cooling foods in moderation.
- Weak person: Add tonics/tonifying foods in moderation.
- Overly strong person: Add regulating foods in moderation.

Dampness is one of those TCM terms and references that at first can be hard to understand and comprehend. One way to describe it is to compare your body's insides to the state of a moldy cupboard, wet, damp, sticky and/or prone to bacteria buildup. Not a nice state to be in. When our stomach, intestines and body condition become "damp" (especially due to living in humid weather), then illness, aches, digestive issues and even mental clarity can be compromised. Foods that exacerbate dampness include bread, milk and dairy, bananas, sugar and honey; foods that eliminate and reduce dampness include corn silk tea (this features in our recipes), barley (Job's tear), celery and asparagus.

Now that you have assessed your constitution, we can use that information in choosing the right foods and herbs to help you achieve and maintain balance. Let's take weak, overly strong and neutral constitutions as an example. If you have a result of a neutral type, it means you are quite balanced. In order to keep this state, it is best to eat a broad range of foods and be sure to drink water according to the climate and your level of perspiration. However, if you have a weak constitution, this means there is lack of material or function inside of your body. You need to add specific foods to your diet, such as jujube (Chinese red dates) or licorice root, to strengthen you and bring yourself back to balance. An overly strong type, on the other hand, would have different requirements for a healthy diet. In this case, foods such as adzuki beans and hawthorn berries can regulate blood circulation and remove undigested food to recover from swelling or bloating of the stomach.

The basis of the "functional food" approach is to match the appropriate foods and herbs to the corresponding body constitutions. As we have mentioned, the body constitution can be overly strong or weak, hot or cold, or mixed. Foods and herbs also have inherent properties; they have different temperatures and tastes, and they enter different channels of the body. The proper use of food can correct the body's extremes, bringing a property that is out of proportion back into balance. It can, so to speak, yin our yang, yang our yin, strengthen our weakness, calm our hyperactivity, cool our heat and warm up our cold to achieve optimal health.

There are many groups and examples of functional foods, for instance:

- Driving out cold: Use ginger and/or lychees.
- Removing heat: Try mung bean sprouts, watermelon, bamboo shoots, or dried chrysanthemum flowers as tea.
- Nourishing and moisturizing: Eat pears and/or bananas.

The beauty of functional food, including herbs, roots, fruits, nuts and seeds, is that it is incredibly powerful, healing, nourishing and defensive for our health. It's also natural and as nature intended. Understanding the power of food and how we can utilize it in our daily life is empowering, energizing and delicious.

6. Three Major Beliefs about Food in Chinese Medicine

Foods and herbs have specific therapeutic actions beyond their temperature, color and taste, or the meridians traveled. A food may either tonify/strengthen a particular substance or function (qi, blood, yin and yang), or it may reduce or regulate the influence of a pathological condition (qi or blood stagnation, dampness, heat or cold). Lychees, for example, reduce cold and regulate blood circulation to treat pigmentation on the face. Kidney beans tonify our yang energy in the body.

Food Being the Cornerstone of Life

Food has regulating, or tonic, functions in the body. It regulates and removes toxins from our bodies, including heat, dampness and cold, and it also strengthens body energy, body fluid and blood, promotes growth, and enhances longevity; it is life-sustaining. Functional food can also help to prevent or treat certain illnesses.

Some Foods Being Harmful or Causing Illness

In some people or under certain conditions, foods can cause acute or immediate reactions and problems. Examples include allergies, food poisoning and symptoms related to lactose intolerance. The timing and amount of food consumption can also negatively impact the digestive system, such as prolonged hunger or long periods between meals, or eating and drinking too much at one meal. Overeating one type of food can also have a negative effect. An example is an individual exclusively eating nuts and seeds may induce oily skin and pimples.

Another way food can be harmful is when people eat foods that don't agree with their body constitution or condition. As we know, TCM believes that individual bodies may be more inclined to have "hot" or "cold" constitutions. Those who are on the hot side may experience more constipation, heartburn or mouth ulcers. If this is the case, they should avoid foods that raise the heat in the body, such as spicy foods, coffee or hot soups. By contrast, people who are in the cold spectrum may have an upset stomach from drinking too many cold drinks or eating ice cream, and therefore should avoid over consuming raw foods or other cold foods that make them feel ill or weaken their digestion, even if they enjoy the flavor.

To avoid excess in eating certain types of foods, you should be mindful of your flavor preference or aversion. Continually eating from only one flavor group can negatively impact various organs. For example, eating only spicy foods can make you sweat too much and reduce water content in the body, making the lungs dry out. Likewise, too much salt can negatively impact the kidneys as they struggle to filter properly. People who eat many sweet things, such as cookies or anything with added sugar, will often face problems with their pancreas from overstimulation and too much insulin production. Maintaining stable blood sugar levels is key to good health.

Undigested Food Becoming Stagnant in the Digestive Tract and Its Harms

This may happen if food is not digested thoroughly the first time, if it is not passed in a timely manner or if particles become stuck in the intestines. Signs that food has accumulated in the digestive tract may include poor appetite, belching or gas with a distinct smell, bloating or diarrhea, and in severe cases, painful heartburn with a bitter taste in the throat and mouth. When not resolved, gastritis, irritable bowel syndrome, pancreatitis and gallstones are likely to occur; polyps can also develop in the colon. To prevent undigested food from accumulating, one should ensure a diet and lifestyle with plentiful amounts of high fiber, whole grains, beans, vegetables and suitable seasonal fruits, and also be sure to chew well at each meal.

Therefore, we need to put all the qualities of food together to fully understand their therapeutic effects.

7. Food Therapy and Seasonal Food

Dietary recommendations are usually made according to the

patient's individual condition in relation to TCM theory. This relates to the "four energies" (hot, warm, cold and cool plus neutral) and "five tastes," which are also important aspects of Chinese herbal medicine. These determine what effects various types of food have on the individual body. A balanced diet leading to health is achieved when the energies and tastes are in balance. When one gets a disease (and is therefore unbalanced), certain formerly routine foods must be avoided or reduced, while some new ones must be added to restore balance in the body.

Our physical and emotional states are greatly influenced by climate and the environment's rhythm and seasons. Our surroundings affect our constitution, whether those influences are physical (such as weather, pollution or seasonal changes) or social/emotional (friends, co-workers and support systems). When we use food to assist our health, we should eat less cold food in the winter, less hot food in the summer, less spicy and pungent food in the autumn dry season and less moist food in the humid summer. Natural environmental influences are not only external, because they affect the water and food we put in our bodies. Therefore, a healthy environment can protect your constitution.

Be sure to select seasonal produce in order to get the most nutrients and health benefits. For instance, some fruits that are seasonal in the summer can assist with cooling the body. Due to globalization and technological advancements in agriculture, some food items formerly available only during the summer may now be purchased year-round. However, this disrupts the natural way and is not conducive to promoting health. Moreover, people should keep their local environment in mind. If you live in an area that is hot and humid, you need to focus on consuming food that can help reduce water retention and cool you down.

Geographical features of a place have a strong impact on both our body constitution and our food choices. People from the north can take more hot food than people who have grown up in the south. People from humid regions can tolerate wet climates better than people from dry regions. In order to get the best quality of ingredients, you should select foods that are still produced in the area from which they traditionally originate. For instance, the best quality goji berries come from Ningxia and Gansu provinces of China. The best jujubes are from Tianjin City and Shandong Province. It is advisable to always look at food packaging to see where the product originates to ensure its quality. Eat locally and seasonally as nature intended.

Additionally, it is important to keep in mind that you can consume larger quantities of fresh produce than dried. Dried produce is more potent and causes stronger reactions in the body.

This tailor-made knowledge helps in judging individual needs when we choose functional food, herbs and supplements. There are so many choices out there, and decisions can often be made on superficial terms, influenced by packaging or advertising. However, if you understand the basics of Chinese medicine and food therapy, your choices will be wiser. With that full awareness, you can allow foods to work holistically and help you get and stay healthy.

Body constitution, food temperature and taste must be considered to choose the perfect foods for you. This book won't provide all the details of these seemingly complicated theories, but visiting a TCM doctor and having your body constitution and condition diagnosed and then eating for your body type will beneficial. As you build your body awareness and knowledge about food and meridians, and as you apply this knowledge day to day, you will see improved health as a result.

Warming and antioxidant rich fruits: longyan, berries, cherries and pomegranate.

Chapter Two
TCM and Smoothies

Though teas, soups and stews are common in TCM, smoothies are not. We have developed a modern-day approach to combining smoothies and TCM food therapy as a wonderful way to explore healthy beverages and your body's constitution.

1. Combining Chinese Wisdom and Modern Convenience

Smoothies have become extremely popular, and rightly so, as people strive to be healthier, consume more fruits and vegetables, and explore superfoods and herbs, all in the context of busier lives and less time. Having a well-stocked kitchen and being prepared to invest time and wisdom into your food and drinks takes commitment and motivation. You will be rewarded, though!

Our goal in this book is to show you how to drink smoothies following TCM food therapy theory, including:

- Using food and other ingredients, such as herbs and natural dried fruits and flowers, to take care of your digestion (especially the spleen and stomach)—otherwise food therapy won't work as well. Many smoothies these days are "one size fits all," and might do some people and some constitutions more harm than good.
- Functional foods combine with different groups to make a strong response because the foods can coordinate with each other. When we use functional foods, we also need to take caution in mixing different foods to be aware of any contraindications.

Through our recipes and sharing our TCM food therapy theory, we trust that you can learn to combine TCM and build your own delicious, easy-to-prepare and nourishing smoothies. We also encourage you to learn more about TCM and the power of functional foods, fruits, nuts, seeds, herbs, roots and spices to achieve balance in your well-being.

2. The Difference between TCM Smoothies and Others

Our TCM smoothie recommendations and recipes have been created with food and health benefiting properties in mind, and then crafted for a tasty and enjoyable beverage you can

27

incorporate into your diet on a daily, weekly and seasonal basis. They involve some "superfoods," including some you may not have heard of that are more commonly used in TCM for healing and restoration of the body, cells and organs.

The main difference between a TCM smoothie and regular smoothie (plenty of which healthful and fabulous) is that they should be selected, prepared and enjoyed according to an individual's constitution. Smoothies are typically a blend of bananas, avocado, green vegetables, cacao, berries, honey, coconut water, Medjool dates, and mango and pineapple for a tropical feel; they are often featured in raw food cuisine. All of these ingredients, while super healthy in the Western wellness scene, tend to be on the yin side (or cold/cooling, contractive) and often include ice, and for **some people's constitutions** and conditions can do more harm than good to an individual's digestion and intestines, especially in the long term. In TCM, warmth and nourishment are key, so we have provided a selection of fun and healthful blends for you to try based on season and your individual condition.

So in summary, the differences between our TCM smoothies and others include:

- Not all are sweet; some spicy and bitter ingredients are included.
- Not all raw—we have quite a few cooked ingredients and brewed teas and herbs blended into our smoothies.
- Neutral fruits: We try to stay as balanced as we can, except for those with strong yang constitutions or those who tend to be more yin and need more yang fruits and energy.
- TCM smoothies require you, the reader and smoothie maker, to live with full awareness about your body type, geographical location for seasonal and available fruits, and blend with your digestion and health in mind.

3. Not a Meal Replacement

While some smoothies are packaged as a "detox" or for weight loss, we have carefully designed our TCM functional smoothies with love and intention for health-building properties. They are not intended as a meal replacement and should not be consumed in place of a wholesome, well-balanced diet. These smoothies will boost your constitution and condition when applied in the right season for your individual body's needs.

Nourish your spleen and warm the digestion with Chinese yam, raspberries, ginger, cloves and cinnamon.

Chapter Three
Preparation

According to TCM and food therapy, different foods have different properties. In designing our TCM smoothies, we have taken into account that it's important to match your constitution and condition according to the season and what effects you want the smoothie to have on your health.

One important note: Please ensure you purchase all your dried ingredients in their natural state, free from salt, sugar, preservatives, colorings and flavorings.

Yes, many of the bases we suggest can be beverages on their own, so imagine the potential at mixing them in with TCM ingredients and super fruits and foods!

1. TCM Functional Liquids and Bases

Let's begin the TCM smoothie making with the bases. As with any smoothie recipe, you need a liquid: We use water, a nut/soy/grain milk, or some brewed and cooled tea.

We have divided the liquids and bases that are key parts in smoothie making into those with cooling, warming and neutral properties. Pick and experiment; explore in different seasons and enjoy the textures, flavors and subtleties our TCM ingredients offer. Once you begin to understand your constitution and feel the effects of the right foods, we encourage you to mix, blend and add according to your taste buds. Our recipes are just a starting point—please play with the beans, grains, nuts, seeds, herbs, flowers, sweeteners, roots, fruits and vegetables.

We suggest trying and experimenting with some amazingly nutritious, detoxing and nourishing liquid bases, such as the following ones we love. Some you may not have even thought of using before, but with the wonderful world of TCM food therapy, we have many choices available to us.

The Cooling Family

Mung bean water. An all time favorite in Chinese and Asian soups, stews and desserts, mung beans are rich in nutrients and vitamins, and they add a wonderful texture and richness to TCM smoothies. The bean water cooled is a lovely summertime treat in itself!

1. Pre-soak ½ cup mung beans in filtered water for minimum of 2 hours (or overnight).
2. Boil in a pot with 3 cups of water on medium heat until very soft and the beans open up (ensure your beans do not dry up in the pot—you may need to add some water).
3. Use the cooled bean water as a nice base for smoothies. Blend the water and beans together as a thickener if you want a creamy smoothie and then proceed with the rest of your ingredients according to our recipes that follow.

Green tea. High in antioxidants and flavor, this is a good liquid base for smoothies. While there are many types of green tea, which we won't expand on in this book, you can pick any green tea type and brand you prefer for the purposes of our TCM smoothie making and recipes. Once you get more into teas, you may opt for higher-quality green tea leaves from China or Japan.

Green tea has a slightly cooling property, bittersweet, helps clear heat and phlegm in the body, and promotes digestion and urination and elimination. It's a popular beverage for summer and detoxing.

1. Boil water and add to green tea leaves/tea bag in a mug.
2. Let steep/brew for 3–5 minutes (time depends on personal preference; the longer you let it steep, the stronger green tea flavor you will get).
3. Let the tea cool and then use it as a base for smoothies, ideally for juice-based or clear smoothies rather than creamy ones.

Chrysanthemum tea. This is a beautiful, cooling tea for summer. Dried chrysanthemum is a common flower used for summer and excellent for hot/yang constitutions and body types. It's a lovely tea for combating anger, anxiety and stress due to its calming properties and its ability to clear the liver (where anger is stored). Chrysanthemum also supports our immune system and relaxes the nervous system, and TCM practitioners have used it for 3,000 years to treat many health conditions.

1. Boil water and add to 3–4 dried chrysanthemum flowers in a mug.
2. Let steep/brew for 4–8 minutes (time depends on

personal preference; the longer the time, the stronger floral tea flavor you will get).

3. Let the tea cool and then use it as a base for smoothies, ideally for juice-based and clear smoothies, not creamy ones.

Millet water. This is a richly textured and flavored liquid that can be used not only in smoothies, but also in savory dishes instead of water. Millet water has nourishing effects for our body and is slightly cooling in nature. Millet is a popular whole grain in Chinese and Asian cooking. Why not try adding some of the millet water, too?

1. Wash and rinse ½ cup yellow millet.
2. Place in a pot and add 3 cups of water (note—this is double the amount of water than if you were cooking the millet for a grain dish).
3. Bring to a boil and cook approximately 8–10 minutes until the millet is soft.
4. Use the cooled millet water/broth as a liquid base in smoothies. Keep the cooked millet for sweet/savory porridges, bean patties and other meals.

Barley water. This liquid is one of the best choices to combat dampness. Use barley water after cooking and cooling in your detoxing and cleansing smoothies (or soups). It's well known in TCM as a diuretic, anti-inflammatory, antidiarrheal, and a tonic for the spleen and lungs. Light in flavor, this is a clear liquid guaranteed to blend well with the cooked barley grains and provide good results for your health. It's rich in fiber, B complex vitamins, minerals and amino acids.

1. Wash and rinse ½ cup barley.
2. Soak for 2–8 hours and discard soaking water.
3. Place in a pot and add 3 cups of water.
4. Bring to a boil; cook for approximately 20–25 minutes until the barley is soft.
5. Use the barley water/broth cooled as a liquid base in smoothies. Keep some of the cooked barley for soups, salads or to mix with whole grains for side dishes and other meals.

The Warming Family

Longan water. A "hot" fruit in TCM food therapy, this is a great one for nourishing the blood and circulation, heart and spleen. Use this liquid as a sweetener; the longan is naturally rich and sweet in flavor, delicious in warming smoothies. Not suitable for "hot constitutions."

1. Wash ¼ cup dried longan.
2. Bring longan to a boil in a small pot with 2 cups of water.
3. Boil on low heat for 10 minutes.
4. Use the sweet longan broth cooled to room temperature as a liquid base in sweet smoothies.

Ginger water and juice. Add a little spice and kick to your smoothies with some ginger; in a liquid form (which we explain later), it's great for warming up your smoothies and contributing a smooth, rounded flavor. Ginger helps to reduce inflammation, is a relaxant, helps reduce cholesterol and expels cold in the body. Ginger is also therapeutically used for strengthening the stomach, warming the lung and digestive system, and strengthening yang.

If you are a hot/warm constitution though go easy on ginger in your TCM smoothies.

1. Peel a 2-inch piece of ginger and slice into pieces.
2. Add to a pot of water and bring to a boil.
3. Boil on low heat for 10 minutes.
4. Use the ginger water cooled to room temperature as a liquid base.

Hawthorn soaking water. Hawthorn berries are nourishing to the blood and spleen, and commonly used in TCM for boosting our circulatory and digestive systems. They help manage blood pressure, insomnia, and anxiety and are a heart tonic packed with antioxidants.

Facing page
Blender: getting ready to make smoothies, get your equipment ready.

1. Wash ¼ cup dried hawthorn berries (usually they come in dried slices).
2. Bring hawthorn berries to a boil in a small pot with 2 cups of water.
3. Boil on low heat for 10 minutes.
4. Use the tart berry broth cooled to room temperature as a liquid base.

Rice/grain water (normal rice/sweet sticky rice). Rice is rich in a complex of B vitamins called "inositol," which helps promote cell growth, slows down the aging process and stimulates blood flow. It's wonderful for beautiful skin, ladies and gents! Rebalancing in TCM food therapy, this is a lovely liquid with neutral flavor, offering a great way to boost vitamins almost invisibly.

1. Rinse ½ cup brown or white rice in water.
2. Place in a pot with 4 cups of water and bring to a boil.
3. Boil for 15–20 minutes until the water is murky and foggy, but the rice is not cooked (we don't want this rice; the purpose is the rice water).
4. Pour out the water and let cool.

The Neutral Family

Jujube juice. This fruit is extremely high in vitamins C, A, B1, B2, protein, calcium, phosphorus, iron and magnesium. Jujubes are high in antioxidants, and help build our immune system and our yang energy/qi. They also support strengthening of our spleen and stomach, nourish our blood and tranquilize the mind. When cooked, the resulting liquid is sweet, rich in color and flavor, and a very versatile ingredient for use in smoothies and in cooking—especially desserts.

1. Rinse 5 jujubes and slice each jujube gently with a knife (slicing either vertically or horizontally across is fine—this allows the sweetness to come out).
2. Bring 2 cups of water to a boil in a pot and add the jujubes.
3. Boil for 10 minutes on low heat.

4. Remove the jujubes (and enjoy them: They are super sweet and delicious, and great for blood circulation).

5. Use the water cooled to room temperature for smoothies, or enjoy it warm as a nourishing beverage/tea.

Adzuki bean water (neutral but often used with cinnamon, or fresh clove to elevate to warming). A popular ingredient in TCM cooking, adzuki beans are earthy, hearty and filling. Adzuki beans and the water contain high fiber, vitamin B, folic acid, and are beneficial for heart care and detoxification. As a liquid base, it's thick, dark red and nourishing.

1. Pre-soak ½ cup adzuki beans in filtered water for minimum of 2 hours (or overnight).

2. Boil in a pot with 3 cups of water on medium heat until very soft and the beans open up (ensure your beans do not dry up in the pot—you may need to add some water).

3. Use the cooled bean water as a nice base for rich smoothies. Blend the water and beans together as a thickener if you want a creamy smoothie, then proceed with the rest of your ingredients according to our recipes that follow.

Corn water/corn silk tea. A traditional Asian home remedy for balancing the body, this liquid is especially good for humid conditions and "dampness" removal in the body. Corn water is a nice base liquid for a summer smoothie.

1. Remove the husk of 2 corn cobs but leave 1–2 layers on and all the corn silk (the "hair" of the kernel).

2. Rinse the corn and place in a flat, wide pot or pan, cover with water and bring to a boil.

3. Boil for 20 minutes on medium heat, turning with a fork or chopsticks every 4–5 minutes.

4. When the corn is cooked and the water is yellow, pour out the water into mugs/glasses and allow to cool.

5. Use the corn water for smoothie bases (you can also enjoy the liquid as a beverage at room temperature/or cold in summer, and it's fantastic for alleviating water retention and removing dampness/humidity from the body).

Natural nut milks: almond, pumpkin and soy bean.

Almond milk. Simply almond and water pre-blended, this is a common liquid base in any smoothie recipe. You can use American almonds or "Chinese" almonds (slightly bitter) in your TCM smoothies interchangeably. Almonds are neutral and sweet in nature in TCM, help with our lungs and large intestines and also provide calcium, which is an important mineral. This is a good neutral base for most people to use in the blender.

1. Pre-soak ½ cup of raw almonds (unsalted, unsweetened, completely no flavor) for 2 hours or more.
2. Blend together with 2 cups of water.
3. Strain with a nut milk bag/fine mesh strainer to separate the pulp/fiber (keep the fiber, and dry for snacks and baked goods).
4. Use the fresh almond milk for your smoothies. You can keep almond milk in the fridge for 2 days.

5. Store-bought almond milk is OK, but find the best quality and most natural one you can.

Pumpkin seed milk. Another neutral and sweet seed, pumpkin seed milk is a nice one to help reduce blood sugar and lipid levels; it is also high in zinc, iron and helps boost our immune system. Pumpkin seeds are often used in TCM to treat spleen and stomach deficiency and clear toxins and parasites; they are also anti-inflammatory. What a powerful little seed and fantastic staple as a milk base for smoothies!

1. Pre-soak ½ cup raw, de-husked pumpkin seeds (unsalted, unsweetened, unflavored) for 2 hours or more.
2. Blend together with 1½ cups of water (the consistency may be too watery or thick depending on the power and speed of your blender, so you may need to adjust).
3. Strain with a nut milk bag/fine mesh strainer to separate the pulp/fiber (keep the fiber, and dry for snacks and baked goods).
4. Use the fresh pumpkin seed milk for your smoothies. You can keep in the fridge for 2 days.

Goji berry soaked liquid. A gorgeous red-orange color, this base will boost any smoothie or juice blend not only in color, but also in vitamin C. A popular ingredient in Chinese teas, soups, dessert soups and cakes, it's now increasingly popular outside of Asia, too, for snacks, in baked goods and breakfast cereals. We love this liquid because it adds a tart flavor but not too sour, as well as an immune system boost.

1. Rinse 2 tablespoons of goji berries and place in a pot with 2 cups of water.
2. Bring to a boil, then reduce heat to low and continue to boil for 15 minutes.
3. Remove the goji berries with a fork or strain out with a tea strainer.
4. Keep the liquid and use in TCM smoothies as a sweet and subtle base.

Liquid bases: delicious flowers, dried fruits and tea leaves.

Other Liquids

Rose tea/water. Dried rosebuds are a very common feature of every tea shop in China and are also available in Western countries. With a delicate flavor, this is a great liquid base for a nourishing and balancing smoothie, suitable for most constitutions. Dried rosebuds are gentle with a bittersweet taste, and have a warming property in TCM to help regulate qi, release stagnation and blood, relieve pain (especially for women during PMS), and help with emotions and mood as they nourish blood vessels to the heart and liver.

1. Soak 4–5 dried rosebuds in hot water and make a "tea."
2. Leave to infuse and brew for 4–5 minutes.
3. Strain and enjoy.

Fennel juice. Fennel is lovely, warm and spicy, and when juiced it gives a real kick to your smoothie. If you are a cold constitution, then fennel can help dispel cold and regulate your qi, and also regulate digestion and help with gas and pain. If you are a warm/hot constitution, note that like ginger, you might want to use this less or not at all as a base. (If you don't have a juicer at home, put a few slices straight in the blender.)

1. Juice ½ or 1 fennel bulb (washed), depending on your recipe and how strong you like your fennel.
2. Use in smoothies as desired, but be warned—it has a strong flavor.

Sea buckthorn juice. A super fruit: If you can buy sea buckthorn juice or concentrate you will not regret it. Wonderfully high in vitamin C, antioxidants and anti-inflammatory properties, it has been used in TCM food therapy and treatments for aiding digestion, as well as treating coughs and circulatory disorders. It's also wonderful for glowing skin, and regular use of sea buckthorn will not only rejuvenate skin, but also boost your immune system.

Sour, astringent and warming, this is great for people wanting to boost their constitution and health.

This one needs to be bought at your health food store or online. It should be 100 percent pure and natural, and super sharp and sour in taste.

Soy milk. Fresh is best and if you can get your hands on a soy milk maker/machine and are willing to invest in one, fantastic; if not, a store-bought soy milk is fine. Select a non-GMO soy milk, unsweetened if you can. As a base, you don't want a strong, overpowering liquid/milk for a smoothie. Soy milk tends to provide a richer and creamier consistency to your smoothie (pending the brand available in your town/country), more so than pumpkin seed milk for example.

1. Make your own according to your soy machine's instructions.
2. Or buy natural (unsweetened) soy milk from your local health food store.

Raspberry green tea smoothie. Please refer to page 119 for the recipe.

2. Flavor Meets Function: Choosing Suitable Foods

Keeping in line with TCM theory, it is important to consider the range of foods and how to balance them in your day-to-day diet, seasonal food intake, and, of course, in delicious smoothies.

Beans and Root Vegetables

We also have a nutritious and carefully thought out variety of bean and root vegetables for you. These require cooking with water to provide a base for your TCM smoothies. These are versatile and excellent for thickening a smoothie! They include:

Mung beans. Cooling in nature, wonderful for summer and hot constitutions, mung beans are used in Asian food culture and food therapy and are a staple food. We use them in our TCM smoothie recipes for a summer ingredient and thickener for those who like a creamy, more substantial smoothie. They just need to pre-soaked and cooked in a pot with water; you can always make a batch of mung beans and keep some for blending in your smoothies. On a side note, save some for other savory/sweet dishes such as bean burritos or Chinese sweet dessert soups.

Chinese yam (*shan yao*/mountain yam). A wonderful healthy starch, Chinese yam is one of the best nourishing foods for our spleen, and to relax and recover from anxiety and stress. To use Chinese yam as a thickener, you need to pre-cook it either by boiling or steaming. We suggest steaming as it's faster and preserves the nutritional value. Be very careful with the hairy skin—it can cause irritation to skin on your arms—so wash quickly, cut into 3- to 4-inch pieces and steam until soft. Peel the skin away and use the white yam flesh as your thickener in smoothies.

Barley. Chinese barley or Job's tears are another key ingredient and super grain in TCM food therapy and Asian culture. This is one of the best, if not the very best, foods for removing dampness in the body and dealing with humidity in summer. It's also a wonderful detoxing grain, and helps melt and dissipate fat and cholesterol accumulations in the body. An all-rounder, we love barley as a versatile ingredient in the kitchen and a nice neutral-flavored thickener in smoothies.

Berries, berries and more berries.

Ingredients and Fruits

As we have learned, one of the foundations of TCM food therapy is the concept of hot/cold properties of food. In this section we highlight some of these that you can use for your smoothies and ones that are suitable for you. It is our hope that once you become more familiar with these ingredients and understand a bit more about food therapy, you take our bases and create new recipes in your kitchen. We haven't necessarily used all of these ingredients in our smoothies but we believe it is important to share the types of foods with these properties with you for reference.

Family	Fruits
Hot/Warming	Cherry, blackberry, date, dried hawthorn berry, jujube, longan, lychee, peach, pomegranate and tangerine
Cold/Cooling	Banana, blueberry, cranberry, gooseberry, grapefruit, lemon, lime, mango, melon, mulberry, orange, pear, persimmon, strawberry and watermelon

Hot/Warming Ingredients

Cinnamon: a favorite but not traditionally used in Chinese beverages.

Cloves: warming, anti-parasitic (a bonus), a lovely spice for winter.

Ginger: wonderful to add some zing and spice to food and smoothies.

Oats: great for bulking up a smoothie and almost making it into a meal.

Quinoa: Add protein and texture with some cooked quinoa, easy to blend.

Walnuts: When blended, these are creamy, smooth and a delicious boost.

Cold/Cooling Ingredients

Aloe vera: Get in juice/liquid form or blend a small piece of fresh aloe.

Asparagus: good for smoothie bowls and/or for some savory options.

Avocado: super creamy and relatively mild thickener for smoothies.

Barley: perfect for summer months and humid conditions, cooks quickly and blends easily.

Buckwheat: summer or mid-season grain, can be used for smoothie bowls.

Chrysanthemum: delicate, light flavor, a lovely way to cool off in summer and hot months.

Cucumber: cooling, refreshing and hydrating, blends easily.

Mung beans: probably the best for summer, the beans add texture; but requires pre-cooking.

Green tea: a popular beverage and great as a TCM smoothie base.

Millet: light, creamy, great in summer as a smoothie thickener.

Radish (long and white): a peculiar one but powerful for detox and cleaning the body.

Facing page

Ginger: grated, sliced, whole and juice.

3. Building Your TCM Smoothie

After all the theory and liquid bases, and information about hot-cold, body constitution and organs, it's time to get ready to build your smoothie (unless you've already skipped ahead to the recipes and begun blending and experimenting). You need to be flexible with the fact that the thickeners aren't like "normal" smoothies or shakes that you may be used to—for example, less water in your nut milk, adding protein powder, or using normal cow's milk—we are using vegetables and nourishing grains to do the job for our TCM smoothies and their creaminess. As for sweeteners, those already into smoothies and superfoods will be familiar with our ingredients, with the addition of jujube.

We also suggest not going out of your way to source a tropical fruit such as a pineapple if you live up in the northern hemisphere where 1) there are no pineapples growing and 2) they have to be shipped a long way away—it's not sustainable and

Anti-oxidant rich nutrients for a green tea, berry ginger and honey blast.

not good for your body to eat foods out of season. We encourage improvising and using logical thickener replacements or sweet/sour flavors if you aren't able to source something in a recipe.

One last thing, on function vs. flavor: Please don't force yourself to add ingredients you don't like or that make the smoothie too strong. Your TCM smoothies should be personalized, made to a sweet/creamy/less creamy balance that your taste buds enjoy. Our recipes and contraindications by a TCM professional are designed to do your health some good, but they are only a guide and a result of creativity in the kitchen.

Sweeteners

There has been much research, data and literature about the negative effects of sugar in our diets and the glycemic index (GI, quite simply an index that measures the effect of foods on our blood sugar level). Especially the hidden sugars in drinks, commercial dairy products, processed food, packaged snacks, sauces, dips, and we certainly don't want to add to the burden when we make smoothies. While dried fruits are high in sugar, from a TCM smoothie point of view (and for our taste buds' enjoyment) we aren't against using some natural dried fruits. Please ensure you buy 100 percent natural dried fruits with no added sugar, chemicals or preservatives.

In relation to the GI we suggest fruits such as berries, apples and pears are best, and then including some local and seasonal fruits in your smoothies. Summer is great for this and your body condition and stomach can handle more raw fruit than in winter. There are also more types of fruit available at fruit stands/supermarkets in summer, for a logical reason, of course. Cross-check our list in the previous section for hot/cold fruits you can mix and match in your TCM smoothies.

- **Honey.** This is a great choice for those with no dampness issues, as the nutrients and minerals inside a good quality honey promote health. A lovely flavor and depth can be added to your smoothies, too, with a natural, creamy honey (for our vegan TCM smoothie fans, please feel free to opt for any sweetener below instead).

- **Brown rice syrup.** A popular option in Japan and Korea and increasingly popular, though newer addition to, the Chinese market, brown rice syrup has a milder taste than maple syrup or honey, and is super versatile to use in smoothies and desserts, too.

- **Jujubes.** These are delicious and add a caramel-like flavor to anything you use them in. Three or four jujubes will do for one portion, and work best if they are pre-soaked for 10–15 minutes before blending. The soaking water is good to use too, so don't waste it!

- **Medjool dates.** This fruit is very popular as a sweetener in raw food and healthy desserts and smoothies, and great for incorporating into your TCM smoothies. We encourage you to experiment and sample the difference in using these dates as opposed to jujubes and see which you like best in different recipes. The soaking water is good to use, too!

- **Stevia.** This sweet leaf is naturally green in color, so please don't be distracted with other colors or versions. The whole dried leaf is best, but otherwise stevia powder is no problem and probably easier to source. A little bit goes a long way with stevia, and remember that it has an aftertaste that you may or may not like. A wonderful option for sweetening your smoothies, though, as it's 100 percent natural and easy on the pancreas, which makes it a good choice for diabetics.

- **Fresh fruits** (according to property and your constitution). Use these in your TCM smoothies when in season and when you need them; our smoothies and recipes do contain fruit but not in large quantities like they would in another smoothie book. We use them as a balancing component, and for flavor (sour/sweet/pungent/nourishing) of a smoothie rather than the bulk of a smoothie.

It's also important to remember that grains, root vegetables (especially yams and sweet potatoes) have natural starches and sweet properties, and our TCM smoothies do contain some of these as ingredients, so we don't use too much additional sweetener. However if you are in transition off sugar, or are a self-proclaimed sugar addict, then you might want to add more honey and sweetener in the beginning while you wean yourself off the sugar levels you are used to. It's better for you in the long run!

Fruits and nourishing seeds and grains.

Thickeners

Easily digestible, super nourishing to our qi and our intestines, high in fiber, protein, minerals and vitamins, check out our TCM smoothie thickener suggestions. Some are also featured in our liquid base section, but actually using the grains and beans in the blender and not just their cooking liquid will produce a creamy and thicker smoothie. The more you put in, the thicker the smoothie will be. Simple.

- **Chinese yam.**
- **Cooked barley** (not Western-style pearl barley).
- **Cooked millet** (yellow millet is cool and sweet in TCM food theory).
- **Cooked beans** (mung beans or adzuki beans are most popular and versatile).
- **Fruits**—obviously, banana, avocado, papaya are going to be your thickest and creamiest options. Anything with a high water content like grapes, kiwi or apples will result in a mushy and perhaps lumpy smoothie, even if you blend well. Our suggestion is to stir as you drink and enjoy the fiber!
- **Nuts and nut milks** (or affectionately often spelt milk in raw food cuisine) are super for thickening any smoothie. Cashew milk is actually one of the best for this job; almond and soy milk are good too. Nut milks such as hazelnut milk or rice milk, even to some extent oat milk, aren't as thick, especially the commercially store-bought ones. Feel free to swap out these milk options with one you like and are able to make/source easily.

Remember: You are creating and following recipes for a fun and nourishing smoothie, not a medicine or punishment. While TCM smoothies are something fairly new with potentially some weird and wonderful ingredients, they are GOOD for you from the inside out.

We have also provided some recipes for smoothie mugs/ bowls, a combination between a liquid smoothie and a porridge/ thick soup. These lend themselves really well to TCM smoothies as our ingredients are so different from regular Western style smoothies and are often quite thick and dense.

So, in order of thickness and to explain this smoothie mug/ bowl concept:

- Freshly squeezed/pressed juice = pure liquid form.
- Smoothie = thicker than a juice and contains fiber, a beverage consumed with a straw or sipped.
- Smoothie mug/bowl = thicker consistency, can be sipped from the bowl or a mug or use a spoon. Not always savory/ salty.
- Western style blended/creamy soup = thick and eaten with a spoon, usually only vegetable based, minimal fruits as usually savory/salty.

Ice

You won't see much ice around here or in a TCM kitchen. Traditionally an extreme cold ingredient, ice isn't recommended in normal beverages, let alone smoothies, as it has a strong effect on weakening the digestion and spleen and in the long term is best avoided. If you have a strong constitution and want a cold drink/smoothie in summer then go for it and add it, or refrigerate before serving, but ice doesn't feature in our smoothies as an essential ingredient.

(Photo by Quanjing)

4. Tools

Apart from the chopsticks (purely for ease of handling things like steamed Chinese yam), small pot for cooking grains, beans and root vegetables, and maybe the tea strainer, most of the tools we use in making TCM smoothies are the same as with any other smoothie. You need a blender; that is unavoidable.

- **Blender:** All the TCM smoothies in this book require a blender.
- **Measuring cups.**
- **Small pots with lids:** We will need to cook grains and beans, as well as brew some ingredients.
- **Strainer.**
- **Tea strainer:** We have a lot of fabulous teas, floral teas, and herbs that need to be strained before we blend.
- **Juicer:** useful for some ingredients and recipes, though not all. You don't have a juicer? No problem—the fruit/vegetable can technically be chopped up and thrown into the blender. It's just nice to have for some things like fennel or carrot juice where the vegetable fiber/pulp is thick and heavy.
- **Chopsticks:** We recommended wooden or bamboo ones, not plastic.
- **Kettle:** Get ready to make some yummy tea and functional food brews!

TCM smoothies and liquid bases, here we come ...

Chapter Four

Recipes

Smoothies are best made fresh, and all our TCM smoothies are recommended to be consumed on the same day you make them to preserve their nutritional value and efficacy. Also, since we're using fresh fruits and liquids, it's best not to refrigerate and consume one or more days later.

The texture and color of TCM smoothies can be quite peculiar to the unaccustomed eye. We are going for nourishment, impressing the body through food therapy and the taste buds through enjoyment, but remember many of the ingredients we suggest are thick and creamy, strong or pungent, and include unfamiliar things. Trust us though, and we're confident you'll enjoy the combinations and the process of blending TCM smoothies in your own kitchen.

Many of the smoothies may not seem like a "smoothie," but by adjusting the liquid bases and water levels you will be pleasantly surprised: Just because a smoothie has grain or beans in it doesn't mean it can't be enjoyed as a smoothie beverage … or turned into a smoothie mug/bowl to enjoy.

We set out to categorize our TCM smoothies by five sections: Nourishing Nutrition, Immune System Strengthening, Detoxification, Refreshment and Digestion Aid. Please note that some of the key ingredients and functional foods that support each section and their properties are listed below. They are also a preview and inspiration for you not only of our recipes but also of your future recipes and concoctions.

For each smoothie we have put together combinations, flavors and measurements that we tested and enjoyed, but as the concept of a TCM smoothie is so new and because we use some ingredients you have never blended before, please remember that sweeteners and water levels may need to be adjusted. Yes, this is a disclaimer; because each of our recipes is a base and we want you to enjoy the smoothies, so make it work for you and your palate!

Lastly, each recipe comes with a contraindication by our TCM doctor. Remember: Health is individual and smoothies should be prepared with your constitution, current condition/ body states and the season in mind.

1. Nourishing Nutrition

Warming: Chinese angelica, longan, lychee, pomegranate and cherry.

Cooling: lily bulb, mulberry and pear.

Neutral: goji berries, jujube, fig, flaxseed/linseed, honey, silver fungus (white Chinese fungus), sweet potato, soy milk and black sesame.

These ingredients and TCM smoothies are for nourishing the body's cells with antioxidants, omega-3 oils and vitamins, and they also nourish our qi/energy stores.

2. Immune System Strength

Warming: ginger, clove, astragalus, raspberry and cinnamon.

Neutral: Chinese yam and licorice root.

High in antioxidants and also anti-inflammatory properties, many of these ingredients also build up our spleen/pancreas, which in TCM is considered the governor of our immune system and good health. Not to mention that they are delicious!

3. Detoxification

Warming: hawthorn berry and rosebud.

Cooling: mung bean, barley, cassia seed, cinnamon, papaya, adzuki bean and corn silk.

Neutral: peach kernel and saffron.

It may seem that everyone is always trying to "detox" or clean their body and lifestyle; well, now you can do so with regular detoxing ingredients, food, fruits, grains and herbs. Just add these into your life more often and be mindful of which ones work for your constitution and condition. Yummy in smoothies while cleansing your organs, just what the doctor ordered!

4. Refreshment

Cooling: mint, asparagus, watermelon and chrysanthemum.

Neutral: plum, olive and papaya.

These are all beautiful and energizing in the hot summer

months. They're light and liquid, clear and refreshing, so try adding these ingredients into your smoothies for a nice TCM tonic.

5. Digestion Aid

Cooling: millet, radish and bean sprouts.
Warming: rosemary and fresh fennel.
Neutral: malt and corn.

For many people, digestion is the weak link in health management and by adding in herbs, restorative vegetables and grains, and reducing digestion-inhibiting foods and lifestyle factors (such as ice cream, fizzy drinks, carbonated water, sugar, stress and anxiety) you can improve digestive function. This is really a key concept to understand—fix the digestion and improve your health for the long term.

Please note that all our TCM smoothies are designed as a beverage only; while many ingredients have TCM food therapy benefits, they are not a replacement for any meals or for any medicine. If you have any health issues or are currently on any medications and treatment plans (either TCM-based or Western medications), please consult your doctor before making the TCM smoothies. Also please note that all recipes are one serve unless otherwise indicated.

6. Summary

TCM principles are a great way to learn about your body type and what foods you need at different times in your life. When you are beginning to learn more about your body and listening to signs of stress, digestive discomfort, cold/heat and many other factors, you can use the power of foods—and in our case the power of TCM smoothies—to adjust your mood and health conditions, while satisfying your taste buds at the same time. One of the other good things about our TCM smoothies is that they get you into the kitchen, where you will most likely have to cook a grain or bean you haven't cooked before. So not only will you have some tasty leftovers to eat for a meal, you will also improve your health from the inside out with tonifying ingredients.

Remember our top tips for creating your very own TCM smoothies and enjoying yourself:

- Never go overboard! Don't go to extremes, with either ingredients or quantities, just because you like something or believe you need loads of a cooling or hot ingredient. You can have too much of a healthy thing and overdose, leading to undesirable results.
- Know your body's internal state and organs, and what you need in which season.
- Don't eat the same things, ingredients or smoothies all year round.
- Every ingredient is a chance to change your health from the inside out—fix the digestion and key organs and you are on track for long-lasting, genuine good health.
- Treat these smoothies as suggestions and inspiration. They do not replace a wholesome balanced diet, and if you have any medical conditions, please consult your TCM doctor or medical professional first.
- Enjoy the process and learning about TCM and smoothies.

Nourishing Nutrition

Lychee, Pear, Flaxseed and Coconut Water

This refreshing tropical smoothie keeps it light with lychees, pear and coconut water, with an added boost of omega-3 from the linseeds. This is a play on typical Chinese sweet soups/desserts but in a TCM smoothie form. Enjoy!If the lychees are too sweet, then add more water; if you have a super sweet tooth and need to add a little honey, do so.

This is a neutral nourishing smoothie with a good balance of pear and lychee—yin and yang—we really love the dash of flaxseed powder for texture, fiber and replenishment. Flaxseed are superfoods that have been used in traditional cultures for a long time, good oils for our cells, hair, skin and nails.

Ingredients

5 whole lychees de-pitted (canned ones are ok but usually come in very sweet syrup so drain the syrup or use less syrup)

⅓ of a large pear

1–2 teaspoons flaxseed powder

1 cup coconut water

½–1 cup water

Optional: 4–5 dried lily bulbs, pre-soaked to reconstitute/rehydrate before blending. These are cooling in nature.

Method

1. Combine all ingredients in the blender and blend together until creamy and smooth.

2. Add more coconut water (going slowly into the blender) if you prefer a less thick and creamy smoothie.

3. Serves 2.

Note: The pear may separate if you leave the smoothie to sit out too long; stir before drinking.

Contraindication

Lychees: If your body feels hot, dry and weak, with heartburn and constipation, or there is an accumulation of yellow phlegm, you should eat with caution—do not consume high quantities of lychees.

Flaxseeds and pears: Those prone to diarrhea should avoid taking too many flaxseeds and pears. People suffering from cold-type cough should avoid eating pears.

Ginger, Pear and Almond Milk

Warm and creamy, this is a nice mild smoothie and easy to make. It's like comfort food in a glass, and while fresh ginger is best, you could try ginger powder if that's all you can find … try a pinch or ¼ teaspoon.

Ingredients

1 teaspoon fresh diced ginger (peeled and rinsed)
1 large pear (peeled, washed and cored)
½ cup almond milk
1–1 ½ cups water (depends how big your pear is and how thick you want your smoothie)
Optional: ¼ cup cooked sweet potato for extra thickness and texture when blending

Method

1. Combine all ingredients and blend together until the pear is well mixed.
2. Add more water if required.
3. Serves 2.

Note: The pear may separate if you leave the smoothie to sit out too long; stir before drinking.

Contraindication

This is quite a balanced smoothie, but please be careful if you drink large quantities in summer.

Ginger: People who are constantly flushed, suffer hot flashes, or have high fever or long-term low-grade fever should not eat too much ginger. Due to its warming nature, people who already have a hot constitution should not eat ginger. Dried ginger is not advised for people who are coughing or vomiting blood or have any other signs of bleeding.

Almonds and pears: Avoid eating too many almonds and pears if you have loose stool/diarrhea, because almonds and pears increase bowel movement, if someone already have diarrhea, better not to eat or eat only small quantity.

Almond, Ginger, Medjool Date, Coconut and Mint

A flavor sensation with sweet, creamy, minty/refreshing and zingy warmth from the ginger all in one glass! If you don't like the coconut flake and "bits" texture, you can try substituting coconut oil.

The ginger and Medjool dates add a good warming effect on the body, and almond milk is creamy and rich, which balances the tropical and light coconut and mint additions.

Try this as a nice afternoon "pick-me-up" and treat at home or in the office.

Ingredients

1 cup almond milk (strained if you are making it fresh. Pumpkin seed milk can also be used, it helps add to the green color of the mint, too)

1 teaspoon minced fresh ginger

2–3 pitted Medjool dates

¼ cup coconut flakes

½ cup water

2–3 mint leaves to taste

Optional: silver fungus (pre-soaked and reconstituted/ rehydrated before blending)

Method

1. Blend in your blender until smooth and creamy.
2. Serve in a tall glass with some mint and coconut flakes if you are looking for a nice garnish.

Note: The pear may separate if you leave the smoothie to sit out too long; stir before drinking.

Contraindication

See previous recipe for comments and cautions of almond and ginger.

Mint: Mint induces sweat and spreads energy out, better not to eat or eat only small quantity if people have dry constitutions or weakness in qi, blood and body fluids.

Pear, Goji Berry and Almond Milk

Sweet and red, this is a light TCM smoothie for which you are likely to have the ingredients in your kitchen most of the time. Remember, the pears can be interchanged with any types of pears that are in season. And if you want a thicker, creamier beverage you can swap the ratio of water and almond milk.

Ingredients

⅓ a large pear (or ½ a normal pear)

1 tablespoon goji berries

½ cup almond milk (soy milk works well, too, with this one)

1 cup water

Optional: ¼ teaspoon ground cinnamon

Method

1. Blend until smooth and the goji berries are all mixed well, giving a light red-orange-colored smoothie.

2. Serve in a glass with some goji berries on top.

3. Makes 2 short-glass servings.

Contraindication

Goji berries: People who suffer from diarrhea or are easily prone to developing mucus in the throat and nose should use goji berries with caution. People who suffer from diarrhea should add cinnamon to this recipe.

Hawthorn Berry, Papaya, Cashew Milk and Honey

This is a keeper—it's a really good skin tonic recipe and full of nourishing ingredients. Papaya has a high antioxidant rating, is wonderful in summer for cooling the body, adding fiber and sweetness to your life while balancing the hawthorn berry's tartness.

Hawthorn berries feature in TCM food therapy and tea concoctions quite a bit, as they promote the health of the circulatory system and heart and help strengthen blood vessels. They are also known for lowering cholesterol and can help reduce anxiety, and the hawthorn soaking water can be used for skin boils, sores and ulcers.

Ingredients

1 cup cashew milk

¼ cup papaya (skin and seeds removed)

3 slices of dried, cut hawthorn pre-soaked

1 teaspoon honey (more or less according to your taste buds)

Note: Papaya seeds are really good for you; they're an anti-inflammatory ingredient and help with digestion, but be careful as they are quite peppery and spicy—very, very peppery and spicy.

Method

Combine in your blender and drizzle with some honey and an extra slice of hawthorn berry if you want to make it pretty.

Contraindication

Hawthorn berries: People who have stomach ulcers or high levels of stomach acid should avoid hawthorn berries or only consume with caution. If you suffer from weakness of your stomach and digestive system or from diarrhea, you should also consume with care. Overdose can cause cardiac arrhythmia and dangerously lower blood pressure. Milder side effects include nausea and sedation.

Honey: While honey is good for the digestive system, when bloated and experiencing diarrhea, abdominal distention, lingering diarrhea, honey should be used with caution.

Sea Buckthorn Juice, Goji Berry, Honey and Soy Milk

One of our favorites, this smoothie is super high in vitamin C from both the sea buckthorn berries and the goji berries. The berries provide some of the highest antioxidants available, are at the top of the superfoods lists and are easy to work with in the kitchen.

This smoothie has a creamy, rich texture with the blended soy milk and is a nicely balanced smoothie providing nourishing properties and something you will want to recreate and enjoy again and again. A great way to drink your vitamin C and nutrients!

Ingredients

1 teaspoon sea buckthorn berry juice/concentrate (2 teaspoons if you like a tart flavors)

1 tablespoon dried goji berries (pre-soaked is best, but not necessary)

1 cup soy milk (unsweetened and preferably a non-GMO soy milk)

½ cup water

1 teaspoon honey

Method

1. Combine all ingredients in the blender and blend together until creamy and smooth.

2. Add more water if you prefer not such a thick, creamy smoothie.

3. Serves 1—it's so good that you may not want to share!

Contraindication

Soy milk: People who suffer from gout or high urine acidity should avoid drinking too much soy milk. Too much soy milk can cause gas; soy milk should not be combined with other forms of protein or sugar as it reduces the medicinal properties and leads to indigestion.

Honey and goji berries: See previous recipes for relevant concerns if you have them.

Black Sesame, Adzuki Beans, Rice Water and Walnut

One of Kimberly's favorites for autumn and winter is this mouth-wateringly good combination of black sesame, beans and jujubes. The result is a sweet, creamy, black sesame flavor sensation.

Black sesames are very different in taste from white sesames; don't be afraid to add more if you like them. They are super good for our hair and nourishing us from the inside out as they tonify our blood and yin energy. Walnuts are considered good for our kidneys, help warm our lungs and treat weakness and low energy during our period of busy and stressful living. Cloves are an option in this smoothie and wonderful for warming pungent properties, and they also promote qi circulation in the body.

Ingredients

- 1 tablespoon black sesame powder
- ¼ cup adzuki beans (add more if you want a thicker smoothie)
- 1 cup adzuki bean cooking water (cooled)
- ½ cup rice water (or add 1 ½ cups adzuki bean water if you don't have rice water)
- 1 tablespoon crushed walnuts (easy to do in a small plastic bag with a big spoon or handle of a large kitchen chopping knife, or use a blender that is dry)
- 4–5 jujubes, washed and pitted
- Optional, but highly recommended: 1–2 tablespoons brown rice syrup or honey
- Optional: ¼ teaspoon clove powder or 1–2 dried cloves
- Optional: 1 teaspoon black tahini if you can get it—it makes the whole smoothie a gorgeous dark grey color

Note: Often easy to purchase black sesame powder in Asian supermarkets, but make sure its 100 percent natural with no added sugar. Or buy whole black sesames and crush/grind them yourself. If you can buy tahini locally where you live, 1–2 teaspoons added in the blender is a real treat!

Method

1. Blend everything together.
2. For a super smooth and well-cooked smoothie or smoothie bowl, cook all the ingredients together in a small pot, let cool and then blend. If you find this too thick, add more water/regular water in the blender slowly until you reach desired consistency.

Contraindication

Black sesame: People suffering from diarrhea should avoid consuming black sesame. Clinical reports claim that in some rare cases, people have allergic reactions to black sesame. Symptoms include itchiness of the skin, cough, asthma attacks, perspiration, upset stomach, abdominal ache and nausea. Consuming large quantities of raw black sesame can lead to obstructions in the intestines. People who have kidney failure, and others who have been advised not to eat foods containing phosphorus should consume only minimal amounts of black sesame.

Adzuki beans: Eat with caution if you have a dry constitution. (Males should avoid eating in excessively large quantities if planning to conceive a baby.)

Walnuts: Those suffering from diarrhea are advised not to eat walnuts.

Cherry and Pomegranate

This is a gorgeous, deep-red smoothie with warming, sweet, sour flavors, perfect for nourishing us. This TCM smoothie is a flexible one as you can use water or a nut milk base in putting it together, depending if you want a clear refreshing beverage or a creamy one.

Boost this with some cinnamon and festival spices during seasonal months and when available.

Pomegranates are a superfood due to their super high antioxidant content; while it is not usual for Chinese to eat the whole flesh and seed of pomegranates (for the crunchy and "bitty" texture), we recommend throwing them all in and enjoying the bits in the smoothie—the seeds are the best part!

Ingredients

⅓ cup seasonal fresh cherries, washed and pitted

3 tablespoons pomegranate pieces including the seeds (fresh or dried is fine)

1 ½ cups water or almond milk/nut milk

1 tablespoon honey

Optional: 4 strawberries, if in season (just to add to the pink/redness to the smoothie and even more nutrients and vitamins)

Optional: 1 cherry with stem for garnish

Method

Add all ingredients to your blender and blend away with a smile.

Contraindication

Cherries: Some constitutions cannot tolerate the iron and cyanogenic glucosides in cherries in large quantities. If over-consumption occurs, make a soup with 200 milliliters sugarcane juice and mung beans, and drink 200–500 milliliters to detoxify.

Pomegranates: Do not eat more than 500 grams because this may induce phlegm and impair the lungs' function. Please note these are for LARGE quantities of these fruits; in moderation there is no problem.

Millet, Goji Berry, Medjool Date and Soy Milk

This is a typical TCM smoothie with its "good-enough-to-eat-with-a-spoon goodness." This smoothie should be a very creamy and milkshake-like beverage, and you can adjust the sweetness by adding more (or fewer) Medjool dates.

Millet is cool and sweet, goji berries are neutral and sweet and also nourish our blood and eyes (high in vitamin C and E, don't forget), and Medjool dates and soy milk—they are just yummy! Enjoy this very relaxing yin TCM smoothie ...

Ingredients

½ cup cooked millet (Yellow millet is quick cooking; cook extra and add to salads or make breakfast porridge, no waste!)

1 heaped tablespoon goji berries (pre-soaked if you want them to blend more smoothly)

1 cup soy milk

3 pitted Medjool dates

Optional: ⅓ cup water

Method

Blend everything together and take to work—this is a filling morning/afternoon snack. Delicious!

Contraindication

Soy milk and goji berries: see previous recipes for relevant concerns if you have them.

Immune System Strength

Chinese Yam, Ginger, Cinnamon and Honey

If you have never seen, cooked nor tasted Chinese yams (literally translates to "mountain yam") then you are in for a treat, and so is your spleen. Chinese yams are hairy, and kind of scary looking, but once handled properly and steamed or cooked, the texture is creamy, lush and rich, and it turns out this ingredient is one of the superstars in our TCM smoothie kitchen.

Your spleen and digestion will thank you for including this in your life due to the nourishing properties for your qi and the bolstering of the spleen function. Together with the honey and ginger, it will boost your antioxidant intake and therefore immunity.

It is a really relaxing and taste-bud-pleasing result (you can thank us later), so have fun and experiment with the ratios of ginger and cinnamon as you desire.

Ingredients

½ cup mashed Chinese yam (steamed/boiled first)

1½ cups water

½ teaspoon grated or diced fresh ginger

2 teaspoons honey

¼ teaspoon cinnamon powder/ground cinnamon

Optional: a pinch of astragalus powder (for superfood warming boost for the adrenal glands)

Method

1. Blend everything together and serve in your favorite glass. This one can be made into a smoothie bowl/mug by adding more Chinese yam for a thicker consistency—and then you can also make more, keep it in the fridge and reheat later. A nice snack or pudding, too, if you get it that thick.

2. Yam preparation: Please note that the hairy brown skin can cause itchy skin/arms, so please don't bring into contact on your arms—stick to fingers, which are much more resilient. Cut the yam into 3-inch pieces, rinse and steam/boil for 10 minutes or until soft when poked with a fork. You will need about 4 pieces of 3-inch yams to yield ½ cup of mashed yam for the smoothie.

Contraindication

Chinese yams: Do not take when suffering from indigestion, a full or bloated abdomen, poor appetite or when the tongue has a thick greasy coating. Eating a high quantity (more than 200 grams) of Chinese yam could lead to intestinal distention. Use great caution with raw Chinese yam, as there have been reports of raw Chinese yam causing food poisoning.

Cinnamon: Because of its blood-thinning properties, cinnamon should not be consumed by people who are experiencing blood loss (for example, due to cough, hemorrhoids, etc.). Due to the warming nature of cinnamon, people who have a fever, acute conditions indicating excess heat (sweating, rash, constipation), cold sores, or pimples on the back of the head are advised to avoid cinnamon. Pregnant women shouldn't eat cinnamon too often; however, it is fine in cooking.

Honey and ginger: see previous recipes for relevant concerns if you have them.

Turmeric, Chinese Yam, Lychee and Almond Milk

With beautiful flavors, a golden glow and creamy yam and almond milk texture, this smoothie boosts your immune system with the dose of turmeric and yam in a glass. And the lychees are high in dietary fiber, antioxidants and vitamins, especially vitamin C. Lychees also are a good source of B-complex vitamins such as thiamin, niacin, and folates, as well minerals like potassium and copper.

If you don't have almond milk or are not a fan of almond milk, feel free to use other nut or seed milks interchangeably. If you aren't into overly sweet drinks, then prepare the smoothie without Medjool dates and add them to taste at the end.

Ingredients

1 cup almond milk
½ cup mashed Chinese yam (see our previous recipe for instructions on how to prepare/handle and cook the Chinese yam)
7 whole pitted lychees (canned ones are OK, but please pour out the sugar syrup it comes with)
2 pitted Medjool dates (pre-soaked if you have any as they blend smoother, but not necessary)
¼ teaspoon of turmeric powder or 1 slice of fresh turmeric root, if available
Optional: a pinch of maca/licorice root powder (for an energy and adrenal gland boost)

Method

Blend everything together and serve in your favorite glass. This is a sweet treat!

Contraindication

Turmeric: Pregnant women should eat turmeric with caution. If you have anemia, and do not have stagnation of qi and blood, then it's better to avoid eating it.

Chinese yams, lychees and almond milk: See previous recipes for relevant concerns if you have them.

Sea Buckthorn Juice, Carrot and Apple

If you are looking for the best source of vitamin C and an instant boost to your immune system, look no further than sea buckthorn berry. Yes, you can look this one up—sea buckthorn berry is a super superfood and very common in natural food products and even skin care due to its immune support function, cell boosting effects, ability to reduce pigmentation and the sheer indulgence it adds to your skin. We are a firm believer in this ingredient and honestly, the next day you will notice a glow on your skin.

Sea buckthorn berry, a Eurasian shrub, comes in juice, concentrate, juice powder, oil, pill/supplement and tea forms, and is grown in Russia, the Himalayas and Northern China. It has a bitter and tart flavor, so if the sweetness of apple and carrot isn't enough for you, add a teaspoon of honey—so good!

We have another recipe in our Detoxification section, but with a few other ingredients added.

Ingredients
2 tablespoons sea buckthorn juice
¼ cup diced carrot (peeled and washed)
⅓ cup chopped apple (red apple best)
1 cup water
Optional: 1 tablespoon honey

Method
Blend everything together, and if your blender is not top-of-the-line, you might want to first grate/juice the carrot.

Contraindication
Carrots: Better eaten if cooked; eating too much raw may disturb stomach function (as with all vegetables in TCM theory).

Apples: Do not consume too much (more than 2 or 3 per day), because it can cause a greasy and tight feeling in the stomach or abdomen. Again, this is in line with TCM theory about balance and not consuming anything in excess.

Blueberry, Raspberry and Rose

This TCM smoothie is arguably one of our prettiest in terms of color and how much edible fun you can have with decorating the glass.

Blueberries and raspberries (and almost all berries) are commonly known for their high antioxidant properties, high nutrient content, and versatility in smoothies, beverages and desserts. Here we pair them with dried rose hips/petals, which are commonly used in Chinese teas and tonic brews, for a very delicate, lightly floral and super tasty smoothie.

Rose is a wonderful ingredient for our skin, immune system, and digestion. It has high vitamin C, A and E content, antiseptic, anti-bacterial, anti-inflammatory and anti-oxidative properties, fights free-radicals and is an aid for PMS. Try this smoothie and you'll be asking why you haven't used rose more before.

Ingredients

⅓ cup fresh blueberries (Frozen are OK, but remember to defrost before using. We don't want ice-cold drinks unless it's summer—in fact, this compromises our digestion and immune system.)

⅓ cup fresh raspberries (Same as the blueberries above: fresh is best, but defrosted ones are an option.)

1 teaspoon dried, de-stemmed rosebuds (save a few petals for garnish on top)

1 cup soy milk or almond milk

Optional: 1 teaspoon honey

Method

1. Blend all ingredients in a blender until frothy.
2. Serve in a nice glass/tea cup and garnish with dried rosebuds (gently crushing the buds in between your fingers for a sprinkling effect).
3. Serves 1; double or triple the recipe if you like it or are sharing with friends.

Contraindication

Raspberries: Do not take if you have body weakness with low-grade fever. Avoid eating raspberries if you are experiencing scant excreta and brown urine.

Goji Berry, Turmeric and Rosebud

Here's a superfood trio—this is a lovely boost of goodness and you can opt to blend for a "smoothie" effect or just drink warm as a tea, really. If you are using turmeric root, though, we recommend blending.

We love all three ingredients so much and can't leave them out of a section on immune-system-building beverages.

Goji berries are staple ingredient in TCM, and turmeric is a wonder root all across the world and features extremely highly in the health food scene (it's highly anti-inflammatory, and amazing for so many conditions and treatments). Turmeric has medicinal properties, helps with our brain health, heart and cardiovascular health and is famous in not only TCM but also in Ayurveda and natural therapies. Rose, as you have seen in our previous recipe, and will see again in Digestion Aid section later, is just a brilliant ingredient.

Ingredients
1 tablespoon goji berries
½ tablespoon dried rosebuds
½ teaspoon dried turmeric powder or 1 slice of fresh turmeric root
1 glass hot water (needed to brew the goji berry and rosebuds)
Optional: 1 teaspoon sweetener (Soaked Medjool date water is really nice here, but honey or brown rice syrup works well, too.)

Method
1. Brew/soak the goji berries and rose in hot water; let cool.
2. Blend all ingredients well. This one can be served warmed, cooled or just as a tea if you want to enjoy all these ingredients as a tea unblended.

Contraindication
See previous recipes if you have concerns about any of these three key ingredients.

Detoxification

Just Rosebud Tea

This is not quite a smoothie, but we had to include it in our Detoxification section due to the amazing health benefits. You're going to like this if you are into high-powered ingredients and balancing your organs in a TCM tea way.

Rosebud tea has been known and shown to clear toxic waste from the bladder and kidneys, it is high in nutrients and helps with digestion (remember our immune system and detox efficiency is all about having good digestion), and can help reduce the risk of diarrhea, gastroenteritis and constipation. And one benefit that we personally love is that rosebud tea can help with our nervous system, so our moods and anxiety woes can melt away. Lastly, rosebud tea helps not only with detox but skin issues such as dry scalp, eczema and psoriasis.

Enjoy this sweet, floral tea with a gorgeous aroma that encourages a calm state.

Ingredients
1 tablespoon dried
   rosebuds
1 cup water
Optional: 2 stems
   saffron
Optional: 1 teaspoon
   honey

Method
1. Brew the rosebud tea with hot water and steep for 5–10 minutes.
2. Drink and enjoy, or use the light-pink tea for other smoothies as a base.
3. You can serve this warm or cold (make more, chill and keep in the fridge in summer for up to two days).

Contraindication
None.

Pear, Green Tea, Wheatgrass and Goji Berry

This is a lovely detox blend with fruit, infused green tea and the well-known detox superfoods wheatgrass and goji berries. Great for strong constitutions and for cooling the body, but in true TCM style we balance the cooling nature of pears, green tea and wheatgrass with some goji berries.

Pears and wheatgrass are cooling, high in fiber, and add a nice sweet touch to this smoothie. Pears bring the fiber and wheatgrass add a big alkaline boost. Wheatgrass is very commonly added in detox smoothies and some of the reasons why include:

- High chlorophyll and nutrients for building our blood, and anti-bacterial.
- High in minerals and vitamins like A, B, C, E and K.
- High in protein and amino acids.
- Cleans and neutralizes toxins and organs in the body, including liver detox.

We combine it here with these ingredients to also help mask some of the grassy flavor of wheatgrass. Enjoy.

Ingredients

¼ of a large pear (or ½ a normal pear)

1 cup green tea (Loose leaf is ideal rather than a tea bag. So 1 teaspoon green tea leaves.)

½ teaspoon wheatgrass powder

¼ tablespoon goji berries (Pre-soaked is suggested if you have time, for ease in blending. Substitute longan for goji berry if in season and this TCM smoothie is too "cooling" for you or results in any stomach issues.)

Optional: 3–5 peach kernels (for an extra detox boost, and to give texture/crunch to the smoothie)

Method

1. Brew the green tea with hot water and steep for 5–6 minutes, then let cool to room temperature.
2. Strain the tea leaves and pour the green tea into a blender.
3. Add the pear, wheatgrass powder and goji berries.
4. Blend until smooth.

Contraindication

Green tea: People who have a "cold or weak" stomach and/or digestive system should avoid green tea. People who have insomnia or constipation should not drink tea. Avoid drinking tea when eating ginseng, poria or iron. Green tea and wheatgrass may be too cool for cold constitutions or those with weak digestive tracts.

Pears and goji berries: See previous recipes for relevant concerns if you have them.

Fennel, Barley, Corn Water and Rosemary

This may be strange combination, as it uses raw fennel, but this is a top ingredient for detoxing. Fennel is high in vitamin C, fiber, potassium, phytonutrients and antioxidants. Fennel has also been studied for its ability to reduce inflammation and protect the liver. Fennel has three parts to it: the bulb, the stems or tops, and the feather-like leaves. We recommend the bulb—pale green and white part of the fennel—either raw or cooked. It's great in a blender, juiced or eaten raw on a salad for detoxing effects.

Fennel is used for many purposes in Chinese medicine, including relieving congestion, stimulating appetite and treating upset stomachs. The fennel seed tea is used for bites, food poisoning and sore throats. In this TCM smoothie we combine it with barley (white round variety, not pearl barley), which is fantastic for cleansing our bodies and adds fiber, corn water (see our Refreshment section for corn water's full health benefits), which is a calming diuretic, and rosemary, for a detox boost.

Rosemary is a great source of iron, calcium and vitamin B6, and is a well-known herb for its medicinal properties due to its high antioxidant content, as well as its ability to help our immune systems, alleviate muscle pain and improve blood circulation.

Detoxing never tasted so good.

Ingredients

⅓ cup cooked barley

⅓ cup fennel juice (If you don't have a juicer, then 1–2 slices of fennel in the blender will work, but the smoothie's texture will be slightly different.)

½ cup corn water (see liquid bases for instructions)

¼ teaspoon fresh rosemary

1 cup water

Optional: Add 1–2 teaspoons of honey or a pinch of Himalayan pink salt, but this is designed as a savory smoothie, or you can turn it into a smoothie bowl with a thicker consistency.

Method

Blend all the ingredients together and enjoy this tonic.

Contraindication

Fennel: People with a mixed dry and hot constitution should avoid eating fennel too much.

Corn: Eating too much fresh corn can disturb stomach function in people with a weak stomach.

Rosemary: Some people are very strongly allergic to rosemary or to the pollen of the flower, in which case rosemary acts more like a poison, so be careful or consult your TCM doctor if you suspect any allergies.

Green Tea, Rosebud, Pear and Apple

Green tea is a wonderful option for cleansing, detoxing and preventing illness. It's a cooling tea/ingredient, so more suitable for warm constitutions and conditions and people with strong digestions. Nothing should be consumed the same all year round (seasonal variety is one key to good health) so save this one for the warmer months.

Green tea provides a powerful and tasty liquid base for this TCM smoothie, while the fruits and dried rosebud bring fruity and subtle tones. Overall, this is delightful beverage for anyone trying to cleanse and detox key organs, especially the liver. Apples and pears provide some fiber, vitamins and a low GI option.

Ingredients

1 cup green tea (brewed and cooled)

⅓ cup rosebud water (soak rosebuds for 1 hour in room-temperature water or 8–10 minutes in using hot or warm water)

¼ a pear, washed and peeled if not organic (use ½ a pear for thicker smoothie consistency)

¼ an apple, washed and peeled if not organic (use ½ an apple for thicker smoothie consistency)

Note: Ginger is a nice complement to this one for either for the zingy and zesty flavor, or a slight warming up of this smoothie, if it's indicated for your current constitution and condition.

Method

1. Soak your rosebuds in water until they're soft and the petals separate.
2. Meanwhile, brew the tea and let it cool to room temperature.
3. Prepare your fruits.
4. Pour and place all ingredients in a blend and blend away!

Contraindication

See previous recipe for notes on pears and green tea.

Carrot, Goji Berry, Green Tea and Flaxseed

What are some of the key elements of an effective detoxification smoothie? We think this one covers a few top components, as it's high in fiber, vitamins A and C, antioxidants, nutrients and omega-3.

Let this TCM smoothie boost your metabolic pathways, adding a load of goodness along the way and providing flavor and satiety as a bonus.

Green tea is also a good one for those who are coffee or caffeine addicts. On a detox, caffeine is often eliminated; rightly so, but green tea provides a nice transition as a healthy alternative.

Ingredients
¼ cup diced carrot (or ½ cup carrot juice if you have it)

1 tablespoon goji berries (Pre-soaked is best if you have time, for ease of blending, but not essential.)

1 cup green tea (brewed, strained and cooled)

½ teaspoon flaxseed powder

Method
Blend all ingredients together and serve.

Note: This is a good smoothie to take on the road as the flaxseed powder is filling and fibrous. Do go easy on the flaxseed for friends and guests as it's a powder; though high in omega-3 and fiber, it could add a consistency that people are not used to. We note that flaxseed will gel up and thicken in liquid, so if you let this smoothie sit, it will thicken over time. Feel free to add water if the flaxseed creates too thick a beverage for your liking.

Contraindication
See previous recipes for notes on goji berries and green tea.

Corn Water, Pumpkin, Turmeric and Ginger

This recipe may sound more like a soup, and this is a perfect example of the smoothie bowl idea. Enjoy the benefits of the cleansing corn water, fibrous and naturally sweet pumpkin, anti-inflammatory turmeric (a superfood) and a dash of ginger for flavor and nutrients.

This is a lovely way to use the corn water (which we recommend making in batches and drinking as a beverage; if you don't like it, then use it in recipes and other experiments in the kitchen). For the pumpkin we recommend using both the cooked and cooled pumpkin water and some soft pumpkin in the TCM smoothie/smoothie bowl. Typically this would be a soup, but the addition of corn water and blending to a more liquid form makes it an easy snack and beverage to take with you anytime in a flask or bottle.

Detoxing with soups (not just smoothies and juices) is popular, so use this as a light meal or snack if you can't treat it as a smoothie.

Ingredients

1 cup corn water (If you are aiming for a smoothie bowl or soup, then some of the cooked corn kernels are a nice addition either blended in or kept chunky and added at the end. We would recommend about 2 tablespoons.)

½ cup cooked and very soft pumpkin and pumpkin broth/water (If you cook a lot of pumpkin, you can use the rest to make soup, puree or desserts—no waste.)

½ teaspoon turmeric powder or 1 slice of fresh turmeric root

Optional: 1 slice of ginger (If you aren't a fan of ginger, feel free to omit it, but it's great for detox and warming and balancing the body.)

Optional: 2 stems of saffron (This offers a detox boosting effect for those who do not have a hot constitution or blood pressure issues.)

Method

1. Blend the corn water and pumpkin flesh and broth together in a blender.
2. Add the turmeric and ginger and blend again until all ingredients are smooth and mixed in well.
3. You can add salt and pepper if your detox program allows and you want to make a detox soup, or keep it neutral and natural.

Contraindication

Pumpkins: If you have stagnation of qi and accumulation of dampness, drink with caution.

Other ingredient notes as per previous recipes.

Mung Bean, Celery and Rosemary

Mung beans are a staple in a TCM kitchen for use in soups, mixed grain and bean dishes, desserts and dessert soups. Putting them in a smoothie or smoothie bowl may seem strange at first, but for the purposes of genuine detox, we have combined them with celery and rosemary for some green cleansing goodness.

Mung beans are high in protein and fiber, low in fat and calories (not that we are advocates of counting calories), and quite the nutrition powerhouse! Mung beans contain a huge number of vitamins (A, B, B6, E, D and K), plus some anti-aging properties that stimulate your production of hyaluronic acid, collagen and elastin. They're not just cleansing—they give you cleaner skin from the inside. Due to their cooling nature, mung beans help with skin conditions such as skin rashes, cold sores, ulcers, boils and pimples, and they're often used when people need a detox of some kind. They're not only a wonder bean in TCM, but also Ayurveda and other natural medicines, and big in the health food world. Mung beans are balancing, and protect through high fiber and anti-inflammatory properties too.

In China, mung beans have long been used for summer desserts and meals, and have been made into noodles, cakes, soups (a popular combination is with lily bulbs and rock sugar as a blended almost-smoothie bowl) and even wine. In the West, we love to sprout them for salads—the sprouts are great in enzymes and nutrition. In TCM, mung beans clear toxins from the body, balance our organs and skin and tonify qi by improving circulation in 12 meridian channels in the body. Talk about functional food!

Ingredients

½–1 cup celery juice (Use more water if celery juice is too strong a flavor for you.)

½–1 cup water (depends on how much celery juice you use, but aim for 1½ cups of liquid for this smoothie)

½ teaspoon fresh rosemary

⅓ cup cooked mung beans

Sea salt: to be tasty

Method
Blend and detox!

Contraindication
Mung beans: Cold in nature, avoid eating these if you have diarrhea due to cold stomach and deficiency in the spleen or suffer from cold hands and feet or poor circulation.

Celery: People who have endogenous cold of the stomach and diarrhea should limit their consumption of celery.

Rosemary: Balances nicely with these cool ingredients.

Sea Buckthorn Juice, Carrot, Apple, Barley and Mint

You know we are advocates of sea buckthorn berry juice, and this is a real treat. We believe that fiber is key for any genuine detoxification, along with nourishing ingredients that provide nutrient value and help alkalize the body, organs and cells. This TCM smoothie is pretty special, delicious and really fun to garnish and decorate with. Enjoy it in warmer months of spring and summer: Watch your skin glow and notice that you feel rejuvenated.

Ingredients

2 tablespoons sea buckthorn berry juice/concentrate

¼ cup sliced carrot

⅓ cup sliced apple

1 cup water

⅓ cup cooked barley

A few mint leaves to taste and 1 for garnish

Method

1. Blend together and enjoy!
2. If the carrot and apple aren't sweet enough for you, add a sweetener of your choice; but if you are making this for detox purposes, we suggest keeping it natural.

Contraindication

Mint leaves: Omit mint if you have a cold constitution or have any coldness or cold stomach/digestive issues.

Please see previous recipes and contraindication notes for other ingredients.

Refreshment

Lychee, Mint and Coconut Water

Tropical and super refreshing, this is a cooling, luscious and perhaps a little addictive recipe. The combination of sweetness, cooling and hydrating all in one is a taste bud and crowd pleaser every time.

Perfect for summer and the hotter months of the year.

Ingredients
5 whole lychees (fresh and de-pitted is best, but canned lychees with syrup disposed will work too)
6–8 fresh mint leaves, washed
1½ cups coconut water

Method
Whiz everything up in a blender. This just might be the quickest TCM smoothie in the book!

Contraindication
See previous recipes especially our note on mint and cold constitutions.

Raspberry, Ginger, Green Tea and Honey

This is the other favorite from our TCM smoothie test kitchen, and it's gorgeous for an afternoon beverage. It's notable not only for its color but also the incredible number of antioxidants loaded into one glass. Raspberry (and raspberry leaf) is one of the top superfoods, great for the kidneys and high in vitamins. Green tea is a versatile tea for smoothies and blends well, and the combination with a tiny bit of ginger really elevates the final result.

This can be served at room temperature or chilled in summer if you have a hot constitution, in which case make more and drink throughout the day.

Ingredients
¼ cup fresh or frozen raspberries (fresh is best in the right season)

½ teaspoon fresh diced ginger

1 cup green tea, brewed and cooled (Tea bags are fine, but loose leaf green tea is the best for flavor and depth.)

Optional: 1 teaspoon honey

Optional: 1 tablespoon *yang mei* plum/ smoked plum juice (This is highly seasonal and may not be easily available.)

Method
1. Brew your tea first or make a pot (to make more of this TCM smoothie) and save some for later.
2. Blend all the ingredients for 8–10 seconds or until you get a nice, light-pink froth.
3. Serve in a glass and garnish with raspberries and/or some green tea flakes on top.

Contraindication
See previous recipes and our notes on green tea, honey and ginger.

Watermelon, Blueberry and Mint

An easy-to-prepare and simple one, but with an impressive and enjoyable result. This has been a summer favorite for a few years as watermelon and mint are brilliant for cooling and refreshing the body in warm and hot months. If you live in a tropical place, lucky for you—watermelon is available, in season and can be consumed all year around. If not, go easy on this popular red fruit in winter, as it's cold and not optimal for that reason.

Ingredients

⅓ cup blueberries, washed

2 cups chopped watermelon

½ cup water (Mainly to ensure the blender blades can catch all the fruit and start the mixing process. Once you start to blend you can add water slowly until you reach desired consistency.)

1 sprig of mint for a real flavor boost, or 3–5 mint leaves

Method

Blend up and enjoy.

Note: This one will separate, so stir again if you are sipping and enjoying slowly or if you make a big jug for a party.

Contraindication

Watermelon: Due to its cooling nature, people with cold or damp constitutions shouldn't eat too much watermelon. Watermelon should only be used in the summer, as the properties are most impactful and relevant then.

Chrysanthemum and Corn Water

Light and clear, purifying and refreshing, this duo of yellow cooling and cleansing liquids can be combined (without a blender even) for a delightful beverage.

There are a few options for preparing this one; either brew the chrysanthemum tea and let it cool and make the corn water separately, or cook the corn kernels with corn silk, and at the end let the dried chrysanthemum flowers brew in the pot. We suggest the first option, as you will most likely have a lot of corn water in a pot and may want to save some for later or another use.

We are highlighting corn silk tea/corn water/corn broth is because it is a little-known secret and one that really needs to be shared. If you live in a humid environment, this is an especially useful and practical beverage to consume, as it helps remove and eliminate dampness and humidity in the body. Not only in TCM—in the West, many urologists and doctors also recommend this as a remedy for kidney problems and kidney stones, and it's a soothing diuretic and helps with bladder infections, as well as reducing fluid retention and urinary tract problems. Corn silk tea is also high in nutrients such as vitamin K, which is something you might not expect when you are making corn on the cob.

The only challenge we foresee is purchasing corn with the husk and silk or "hair" still intact. A good organic store or farmers market would be your best bet. We also try to get our corn from our regular organic farm and they know to leave the corn whole.

Traditionally brewed in summer, chrysanthemum tea is so well ingrained in Chinese and Asian culture you can even find packaged drinks in this flavor, just note they have sugar and aren't as natural as a fresh cup or pot you make at home. It's purely dried chrysanthemum flowers and hot water; please use about 2–3 flowers per cup per person. The flowers expand in the water and too much could be lead to overdosing and too much cooling of the body and stomach. This tea is caffeine-free, lovely and cool and refreshing for warmer months.

Ingredients
2–3 chrysanthemum flowers
2 corn cobs with the silk/hair intact

Method
1. Brew chrysanthemum flowers in hot water.
2. Wash, then boil the 2 corn cobs with the silk/hair intact for 20 minutes in a wide and deep pot, until the water turns yellow like the color of apple juice. Let cool to room temperature before drinking or mixing.
3. Pour ½ cup of each liquid together for a refreshing beverage. This is not a smoothie but is a great combination to refresh, cleanse and detox the body. Not bad for such simple yet effective ingredients.
4. Can be served chilled in summer if you prefer, but don't forget to be careful of ice (too cold on the spleen).

Note:We suggest eating the corn, slicing the kernels off for salads and vegetable dishes, or even freezing for future use.

Contraindication
Chrysanthemum: People with bladder problems (too much or too frequent urine) should avoid chrysanthemum. And while this could be too much medical/personal information, it's important—men experiencing accidental seminal emission problems and/or having disturbed dreams are advised not to consume chrysanthemum. You've got to love the practical application of TCM!

123

Asparagus Smoothie Bowl

Asparagus is another TCM wonder for removing dampness and excess fluids in the body. We are a fan of dampness-removing ingredients as Shanghai, where we live, is a pretty hot place in summer and incredibly humid all year around, so let us help you if you, too, live somewhere humid.

Asparagus is a nice source of fiber and protein, which are essential for optimal digestion and immunity, and this smoothie bowl/soup is a lovely one for summer or served hot in winter. Asparagus contains many anti-inflammatory compounds as well as antioxidants, including glutathione, which is highly respected for protecting our skin from sun, pollution and aging. High in folic acid and vitamin K, asparagus is also good for our bones, kidneys and intestines, plus it reduces blood clotting, and helps manage blood sugar with its vitamin B content. Asparagus juice has loads of potassium too. Be mindful that bananas are "damp" as a fruit, so if you eat a lot of them and have trouble with dampness (see your TCM practitioner) then asparagus is a good remedy for managing that.

We could really go on about the mighty asparagus, but lastly— it's got the flavonoids quercetin and kaempferol, both plant-based substances and antioxidants that fight inflammation-related diseases.

Ingredients

1 cup chopped asparagus, washed (approximately 4 spears asparagus)
½ cup sliced carrots, peeled and washed
½ an apple, washed, peeled and sliced
1 tablespoon lemon juice
2 cups water
Optional: 1 teaspoon honey/sweetener

Method

1. Briefly steam or boil the asparagus for 2 minutes until they change color but aren't soft or overcooked. Let cool.

2. You can steam or boil the carrots, too, but raw is fine if you have a good blender. If you do cook them, let cool to room temperature.

3. Blend the asparagus, carrot and 1 cup water (using some of the steaming water is a good idea, too, once cooled—no waste).

Note: If you want to turn this into a more savory smoothie bowl or a watery soup, add some salt and pepper and mild herbs. In this case, dried dill or dried parsley is nice. Mint could work, too, for summer months.

124

Contraindication

Asparagus: People who have a weak spleen or "cold stomach" should mix asparagus with garlic or only eat small amounts.

Digestion Aid

Corn Water, Rosemary, Sprout and Barley

Maintaining good digestion is key to optimal health, as our stomachs and intestines govern our ability to fight off illness, viruses, colds and bacteria; ensuring we have cleansing and bulk-forming fibrous foods every day is a good way to live. An overly acidic state, which is common in the modern day diet with lots of dairy, meat, refined carbohydrates, sugar and chemicals/preservatives, brings a host of problems to our health. Many smoothies and juice diets aim to correct this, and they do brilliantly. However, according to TCM food theory, they can do our digestion some mild harm. Coldness and dampness need to be managed and constantly balanced, and having some cooked ingredients like we have shown you in our recipes and liquid bases is one way to restore the stomach.

This savory smoothie bowl is a great one for settling the stomach, removing dampness and adding alkalinity to the body. We explained each ingredient earlier, but this combination has been filed for digestion due to its fibrous nature, delicious creamy blend with the barley, and of course two powerful dampness-removing ingredients (corn water and barley).

The addition of sprouts brings enzymes to this smoothie bowl, as well as a different texture and a boost of nutrients. Sprouts are one of Kimberly's favorite things; they signify freshness, healthiness and are super alkaline—the state we want our body to be in.

Ingredients

1 cup corn water
1 teaspoon fresh rosemary sprigs
¼ cup fresh sprouts (Pea shoot sprouts work really well; other options like alfalfa are fine, but tend not to blend well, as they are thin and may get stuck in your blender.)
½ cup cooked barley
A pinch of sea salt to taste

Method

1. Prepare your corn water and barley in separate pots (boiled and cooled).
2. Blend all ingredients together in your blender, season with salt and enjoy.

3. If you want to make a big batch of this as a smoothie bowl/soup, then save some rosemary and corn kernels for garnish. Yum!

Contraindication
See previous recipes for notes and cautions for various constitutions.

Millet, Radish and Corn Smoothie Bowl

Millet is a really nourishing grain; it cooks quickly and has a wonderfully mushy and soft texture perfect for blending and thickening. Radish adds a kick in flavor and beautiful pink-red color, and the corn water is a nice base for bringing it all together.

Small red baby radishes contain the same properties as the long white ones we have been using for removing dampness, but the spice and pungency of the little red ones are preferred for this dish—they have a different flavor.

Millet is a cool, sweet grain in TCM food therapy and used more in spring and summer months as a lighter grain option. The sweet properties also help balance our blood sugar levels. Remember: Good health and management of weight and cravings is all about balancing our blood sugar. Using millet and other sweet grains and sweet root vegetables is one of the best and most natural way to balance your diet, pancreas and insulin levels.

Feel free to season with some salt for a savory bowl, and get your spoon ready to dig into this one.

Ingredients
2 cups corn water (prepared as previously shown)
2 small red baby radishes, washed and chopped roughly
½ cup cooked millet
Optional: salt and your favorite dried herbs

Method
Blend it all up and serve in a shallow bowl. Great for breakfast served warm.

Contraindication
Radishes: People who have qi and yang weakness, or have a dry and weak constitution without indigestion and accumulation of phlegm, should avoid eating too much radish. Do not combine with ginseng, as radish can reduce the qi strengthening properties of ginseng.

Millet, Fennel and Mung Bean

Millet, detoxing fennel and cooling mung beans create a delicious creamy blend of whole grains. This is a wonderful smoothie for summer and/or those with yang and hot conditions.

Millet is on the cooling side of food therapy, and you combine it with the highly detoxing fresh fennel juice and mung beans, you have a pretty nice drink. If you want to add some sweetener, please go ahead with a dash of your favorite healthy sweet (see the list of sweeteners on pages 50 and 51). A teaspoon of honey is nice for this TCM smoothie.

Ingredients
½ cup cooked millet
½ cup fresh fennel juice
(or ¼ a fresh fennel bulb washed and sliced)
⅔ cup cooked mung beans
1–1 ½ cups water

Method
1. Combine all ingredients in the blender and blend together until creamy and smooth.
2. Add more water (going slowly into the blender) if you prefer not such a thick creamy smoothie.

Contraindication
Millet: If eaten in normal quantities, 10–30 grams is fine; children lacking appetite should drink minimally or avoid.

See previous recipes and our notes on fennel and mung beans.

Millet, Medjool Date and Sea Buckthorn Juice

Millet is a key feature in this section; it blends well and we love using it, but feel free to use other grains if you are concerned about the cool nature of it. You could substitute with oats or soft-cooked brown rice or quinoa. Quick-cooking oats are suggested over rolled oats or steel-cut oats, which are raw and have pieces that are too big and thick.

The combination or rather opposite flavors of the sweet Medjool dates and sour sea buckthorn juice/concentrate bring a nice depth to this one and this can quite easily be made as a TCM smoothie or a smoothie bowl all depending on how much water you add during the blending process.

Ingredients
½ cup cooked millet
2 tablespoons sea buckthorn berry juice/concentrate
3 Medjool dates, pitted
1 cup water

Method
1. Cook your millet (approximately ⅓ cup raw millet boiled in 1 cup of water). Or use leftover millet—yes, we recommend always having some nice cooked grains in the fridge for cooking, using in salads and side dishes, making bean patties with, and of course for your TCM smoothies.
2. Blend all ingredients in your blender and enjoy. Adjust the sweetness once you've made and tasted this smoothie— then you'll know if your taste buds want an extra Medjool date or two.

Contraindication
Medjool dates: Do not eat or eat with caution if you have accumulation of dampness, any phlegm, or indigestion with food. Also avoid if you have been diagnosed with worms/parasites or decayed teeth.

Adzuki Bean and Papaya

You may have many reasons for picking up this book, but if one of them is to add more fiber into your diet through smoothies, then this smoothie is for you! Very high in fiber, with warming and nourishing ingredients, this is a delicious, almost desert-like one.

One note about papaya seeds is that they are extremely peppery/spicy and not often used in smoothies, desserts nor food BUT they are incredibly good for the digestion and reducing any shock or inflammation in the body and gut. You are free to try some in this smoothie, but be warned that they are peppery. On the other hand, if you are needing them then check online how fabulous they are and proceed at your own peppery risk.

Ingredients

½ cup cooked adzuki
  beans (cooked like
  any of our other
  grains/beans)
1 cup adzuki bean
  cooking water (or
  water if you already
  used/discarded your
  bean water)
¾ cup water
½ cup papaya flesh,
  cut and sliced, seeds
  removed

Method

1. Blend away and enjoy this thick and rich
TCM smoothie!
2. As usual, you can water it down with
more water or adzuki bean water, yum.

Contraindication

See previous recipes and our notes on the
ingredients.

Hawthorn Berry and Fig

Hawthorn berries are a popular dried ingredient in TCM treatments, teas and concoctions. They help lower cholesterol, contain powerful antioxidants (which boost our blood flow, fight illness and keep us healthy on the inside), and keep our food in the stomach—if you suffer for tummy upsets or bugs, this could help. Hawthorn berry also helps break up fats and greasy foods, so this is a bonus in recovering your digestive tract, and many people turn to this super fruit in times of indigestion, diarrhea, and stomach pain.

On a more holistic nutrition note, hawthorn berry is often used to reduce anxiety, as a mild sedative, to aid in better sleep, to increase urine flow, and even for women's menstrual problems. Hawthorn berry tonics, teas and broths are used for skin sores, itchiness and warming up extreme cold conditions like frostbite.

We are keeping it light with this TCM blend. You could just boil water and brew dried hawthorn berry slices (available at all TCM dispensaries and Chinese stores/tea shops), but blending with fresh figs—which are very high in fiber, sweetness and goodness—creates a delicious treat in the mouth and belly.

Ingredients
¼ cup dried hawthorn berry slices or approximately 5–6 pieces
2 fresh figs, washed and stem removed, chopped in quarters to throw in the blender
2 cups water

Method
1. Boil your water and steep the hawthorn berry slices in it for 5–10 minutes.
2. Strain the hawthorn berries and let the liquid cool (now you have hawthorn tea, a sour, tart beverage that isn't fabulous on its own).
3. Blend the hawthorn liquid (with 2–3 of the soft, expanded hawthorn berry slices) and fig in a blender until smooth.
4. Serves 3–4 people and keeps well in a jug or flask.
5. The figs should add plenty of sweetness, but if you really want more, then go for it with some honey or brown rice syrup.

Contraindication

Hawthorn berries: There are raw hawthorn berries and cooked hawthorn berries, and if you have indigestion, it's better to choose cooked or boiled hawthorn berries. Raw hawthorn berries can be used for helping blood flow.

Figs: If your stomach is adverse to cold drinks or feels cold pain easily, eat figs with caution.

Appendices

Acknowledgement

A few happy snaps of our contributors, taste testers, supporters, photo genius, stylists and team are as below. Thank you all so much for your patience, honesty and enthusiasm during our TCM smoothie creating process.

And if you, the reader, are ever in Shanghai, please do come by the Sprout Lifestyle store, demo kitchen and nutrition cooking school. In our café you may just find some of these TCM smoothies on our seasonal menu (www.sproutlifestyle.com).

Vivian and Kimberly food styling in Sprout Lifestyle café.

Rosa the food styling and photographer.

Jieli enjoying a sneaky smoothie taste.

Recipe testing … here we go!

Cheryl & Franziska recipe testing in the kitchen.

Rosa getting the angle and smoothie shot right.

Index